Windows XP:
An Introduction

Windows XP:
An Introduction

Stephen L. Nelson

BARNES
&NOBLE
BOOKS
NEW YORK

2002 Barnes & Noble Books

Book design by Lundquist Design, New York

ISBN: 0-7607-3147-0

Printed and bound in the United States of America.

02 03 04 05 MP 9 8 7 6 5 4 3 2 1

Contents

Introduction

Before you skip this Introduction and turn to Chapter 1, there are two things you should know. First, you should know a little about the design of this book. Second, you should have a basic understanding of what Microsoft Windows XP is. So I'm going to discuss these two topics first.

About This Book

Let's start by describing the four things you'll want to know: what this book assumes about your computer skills, how this book is organized, what conventions I've used here, and what I've assumed about the way you've installed Windows XP.

What This Book Assumes About Your Computer Skills

This book assumes you're either a beginning or an intermediate user of Windows XP. To use this book, for example, you don't need to have any special computer knowledge. So *Windows XP: An Introduction* can work rather nicely for beginners—people who are new to computers and to the Windows operating system. By the way, if you are a beginner, read the first three chapters to get the background information you need to start.

If you've already worked with a previous version of Windows a bit, or if you've already experimented with Windows XP, you can also use this book to learn everything you need to know to use Windows XP on a daily basis—and a bit more. So *Windows XP: An Introduction* also works well for people who want to possess a good, general working knowledge of Windows XP.

You should know that you don't have to read this book from cover to cover. You can. But you don't have to. For example, you can use either the table of contents or the index to look up a topic you're confused about or one that's causing you trouble. Then you can dip in, read a few paragraphs to answer your questions, and get back to work.

One other thing you should know right from the start. This book covers the high points of Windows XP, providing you with the essential information you need and then making a suggestion as to the best way to carry out a specific task. In this way, I hope to save you time and reduce your head-scratching.

If you want to become a power user, you'll need more information than this book provides. Sure, this book is a great place to start. But there's more to working with Windows XP than I can cover in just over a couple hundred pages.

How This Book Is Organized

Windows XP: An Introduction has eleven chapters and two appendixes:

- Chapter 1, "Starting Windows XP," talks about how you start Windows XP, explains what the Windows desktop is, and tells you how to start and stop Windows programs after you've started Windows XP. If you're new to Windows, read this chapter first.

- Chapter 2, "Windows, Commands, and Dialog Boxes," explains how you choose commands and work with dialog boxes.

- Chapter 3, "Files, Folders, and Disks," provides a straightforward discussion of how you use Windows XP to create, manage, and store information using files, folders, and disks.

- Chapter 4, "Printing," supplies easy-to-apply information and advice about how you use Windows XP to print documents.

- Chapter 5, "Communicating on the Internet," tells you everything you need to know to connect to the Internet, use e-mail, and work with newsgroups. Chapter 5 also talks about instant messaging.

- Chapter 6, "Sharing Information Over the Internet," explains how to work with the World Wide Web.

- Chapter 7, "Windows XP Accessories," describes how to use the free accessory programs that come with Windows XP, including Calculator, Notepad, Paint, and WordPad. It also discusses the Program Compatibility Wizard.

- Chapter 8, "System Tools," explains how to use Windows XP system management tools.

- Chapter 9, "Troubleshooting Windows XP," helps you solve problems by explaining how to use Help and Support Center, how to use Windows XP troubleshooters, and how to get online support through the Internet.

- Chapter 10, "Customizing Windows XP," provides step-by-step instructions for adding new hardware, installing and uninstalling programs, and making other changes to the way that Windows XP works.

- Chapter 11, "Entertainment, Sounds, and Games," talks about how to use Windows XP for running multimedia programs, listening to music, and playing computer games.

Windows XP: An Introduction also includes two appendixes:

- Appendix, "Installing Windows XP," gives you information about the various ways to install Windows XP and walks you through steps to prepare for installation.

- The Glossary lists technical terms that are sometimes confusing to new users.

Conventions Used Here

This book uses a handful of simple conventions for presenting information. So let me explain them before you dive in.

Sometimes, over the course of a chapter, a piece of information is relative to the topic but it interrupts the flow of the discussion. When this happens, I'll set that information apart as a "Note."

A Note provides backup information that's related to the general discussion at hand but is not critical to your understanding. A Note also provides a cross-reference to other chapters where additional, related information appears. Notes offer tips or advice or present information that can save you time and trouble. Notes will also offer warnings to alert you to potential trouble spots.

Here's another convention I've adopted. When I refer to some button or box on a window or dialog box, I'll capitalize the item's name. For example, some dialog boxes have a box that's labeled "Print to file." If I want to tell you to click this box, however, what I'm going to write is, "Click the Print To File box." Okay? This isn't a perfect gambit. But what I'm hoping is that you'll see the capital letters, remember reading this paragraph, and say, "Oh, I understand. 'Print To File' is the label next to the check box."

Finally, note that this book includes a Glossary. The first time I use an important technical term in a chapter or even in this Introduction, I'll boldface the term to alert you that the Glossary provides a definition for the term. Take, for example, the term operating system. Because that's an important term, I'll boldface it the first time it appears in a chapter. (I'm going to start following this convention in the remaining paragraphs of this Introduction, too, now that I've told you about it.) That way, if you don't know what an operating system is, you can flip back to the Glossary and look up the definition.

Note I'll talk more about operating systems a little later in this Introduction.

An Assumption About the Way You've Installed Windows XP

This book makes an assumptions about the way in which you've installed and set up Windows XP. It assumes that you haven't switched the way your mouse buttons work. In other words, I assume you click your mouse by pressing the left mouse button. And to indicate that you should click your left mouse button, I just say, "Click." If I want you to instead click the right mouse button, I say, "Right-click." Most people's mice will work in exactly this way. But if you've flip-flopped the traditional way the left and right mouse buttons work, you'll need to mentally edit my instructions.

What Is Windows XP?

Windows XP is an operating system, and it is the latest version of Windows. Its predecessors included Windows 3.x, Windows 95, several versions of Windows 98, Windows NT Workstation, and Windows 2000 Professional. Windows XP comes in two flavors: Home and Professional. Windows XP Home is designed for consumers (home users), and Windows XP Professional is designed for business users.

Strictly speaking, Windows XP Professional is a superset of Windows XP Home. In other words, everything you'll find in Home, you'll also find in Professional. But Professional contains additional features that concern security, networking, and administration. With few exceptions (and I've pointed them out in the text), everything in this book will work on both Home and Professional.

What's New in Windows XP?

You may have bought this book or be thinking about buying this book because you've bought a new computer that came with Windows XP already installed. Or you may have picked up this book because you're thinking about upgrading to Windows XP or buying a new XP computer. In either case, you'll probably find it helpful to know about some of the new features in the operating systems, all of which I discuss in this book. The following descriptions are not an exhaustive list of every new feature but those that the intended users of this book will want to know about.

The Start Menu and the Desktop

The Start menu has been redesigned to be easier and quicker to use. The desktop is cleared of clutter. If you do a clean install on a newly formatted hard drive, the only item you'll see on the desktop is the Recycle Bin. Of course, if you bought a new computer that came with Windows XP, the manufacturer of that computer could have put any number of items on the desktop.

Control Panel

Control Panel has also been redesigned. When you first open it, you'll see a new interface and categories from which you can choose applets. The purpose of this new design is primarily to make access easier for new users of Windows. But the Classic view of Control Panel is still available, and if you're an experienced Windows user, you can easily revert to it.

Windows Media Player Version 8

Windows Media Player Version 8 is a vast improvement over even its immediate predecessor. If the multimedia capabilities of your computer are important to you, you'll be pleased with the new version of Media Player. It includes a video and DVD player, a CD player, an Internet radio tuner, and a jukebox for playing and organize video and audio files.

Windows Movie Maker

Movie Maker is a program you can use to capture video, edit video and audio, and create video files. You can also use it to create slideshows with still images.

CD Burning

If you have a writeable CD drive, you can use the feature built in to Windows XP to copy (burn) files from your computer onto a CD. These files can contain music, text, images, and so on.

Help and Support Center

The Windows XP help system is radically redesigned and improved. You can access information on your local system, connect to Internet support sites, access newsgroups specifically devoted to Windows XP topics, and even get remote assistance from a friend or colleague.

Wizards

Windows XP includes a number of wizards (step-by-step guides) that walk you through everything from connecting to the Internet to installing new hardware, including scanners and digital cameras, to installing Windows XP.

Chapter 1

Starting Windows XP

Getting started with any operating system is always a little tough. You can even feel as if you're being taught to swim by being thrown off the end of the dock. To make sure that I don't do that to you here, however, let's start our discussion with four basic subjects:

- Starting Windows XP
- Switching from One User to Another
- Exploring the Windows XP desktop
- Starting and stopping Windows programs
- Stopping Windows XP

Starting Windows XP

To start Microsoft Windows XP, you simply turn on your computer. That's it. Your computer, as it starts, automatically starts Windows. You'll see the Windows startup screen briefly. What happens next depends on how your computer is set up, whether multiple users use the computer, whether you are working on a standalone machine or a network, and, if you are working on a network, whether that network is part of a workgroup or a domain. In any of these situations, starting Windows XP is referred to as logging on. Logging on in Windows XP is really easy, but the process is different from that in previous versions of Windows. For one thing, more than one user can be logged on to a single Windows XP machine at the same time. (I'll talk about that in detail later in this chapter.)

Logging On

Let's start by looking at how you log on if you are working on a standalone machine or part of a Workgroup network. In most cases, you'll see a Welcome screen similar to that in Figure 1-1 (next page). To start Windows XP, simply click your user name. By default, user accounts are not set up with passwords, but if you set up your system so that users are required to log on with a password, you'll next be prompted to type the password. Do so and press Enter to start Windows XP. If someone has turned off this screen, you may see the classic Log On to Windows dialog box instead.

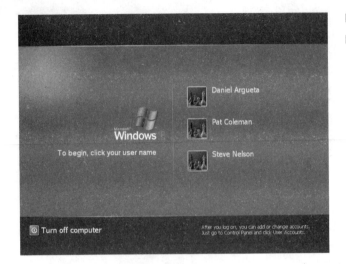

FIGURE I-I

Logging on to Windows XP.

Note If Windows XP was already installed on your computer when you bought it and your computer is not part of a network, you may see neither the Welcome screen nor the Log On to Windows dialog box but the Windows XP desktop instead.

If you work on a network—say your computer connects to other computers because you work in an office—your computer may be connected to a domain. A domain can be the description of a single computer, a department, or a complete network and is used for administrative and naming purposes. When your computer is part of a domain, you'll see a Windows Log On Screen when you first turn on your computer. Press Ctrl+Alt+Del to display the Log On to Windows dialog box. Enter the user name and password that your network administrator assigned to you, and press Enter.

Logging Off

Logging off in Windows XP is also a simple task, but you'll want to be aware that logging off Windows XP and stopping Windows XP are not the same thing. When you log off, Windows XP closes all the programs and files you've been using. If any file contains unsaved changes, Windows XP prompts you to save the file. Stopping Windows XP means powering down your computer, and I'll show you how to do that in the last section of this chapter.

To log off, click the Start button, and then click the Log Off button to display the Log Off Windows dialog box, as shown in Figure 1-2. Click the Log Off button.

FIGURE 1-2

Logging off Windows XP.

> **Note** When might you want to log off? If you work in an office with other people, you might want to log off when you go to lunch or are otherwise going to be away from your computer for a period of time. If your computer is password protected, only someone who knows your password can then log on as you and have access to all your files and programs. If you aren't running programs that need to continue, you might want to log off to allow another user of the computer to log on.

Switching from One User to Another

As I mentioned earlier, multiple users can be logged on to a Windows XP computer at the same time. Obviously, only one user can be physically seated at the keyboard and working, but other users can have programs running and files open. For example, I can log on, begin to download a large file, and then turn my attention to a non-computer-related task. Another user who has an account on my computer can then log on to the system and begin to enter figures in a database program. As you might suspect, there are advantages and disadvantages in such a situation. When you switch users rather than logging off, tasks that are in process continue to run rather than being halted. But as you might expect, your computer will need to be equipped with extra horsepower. If you plan for two or three users to be connected simultaneously and running programs, you'll need at least 256MB of RAM.

To switch users, follow these steps:

1 Click the Start button, and then click the Log Off button to open the Log Off Windows dialog box.

2 Click the Switch User button to open the Welcome screen.

3 Click the user name under which you want to log on, and supply a password if necessary.

Exploring the Windows XP Desktop

After you successfully start Windows, you will see the Windows desktop on your monitor (see Figure 1-3). The Windows XP desktop is the starting point from which you begin any task in Windows. You use it to start and stop programs (as I'll talk about later in this chapter). You use it to stop Windows. And you can use it to open document files you've created with a program such as your word processor. For these reasons, you'll need to understand the key parts of the desktop.

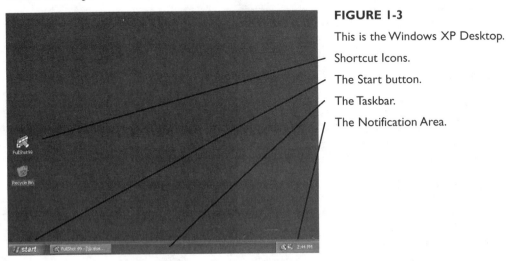

FIGURE 1-3

This is the Windows XP Desktop.

Shortcut Icons.

The Start button.

The Taskbar.

The Notification Area.

The first and most important element of the Windows desktop is the Start button, which is located in the lower-left corner of the screen. You use the Start button to start programs. To use the Start button, move the mouse so that its pointer rests on the Start button. Then click the mouse. When you do this, Windows displays the Start menu (shown in Figure 1-4), which lists several items you can start.

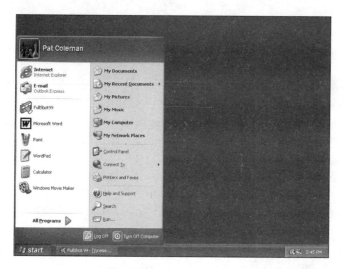

FIGURE 1-4

The Windows XP desktop showing the Start menu.

The items on the left side of the Start menu vary according to which programs are installed on your computer and which programs you have most recently used. For example, if you use a Web browser other than Internet Explorer, that browser's name might appear under Internet. If you use an e-mail program other than Outlook Express, that program's name might appear under E-mail. (You'll see how to specify the programs shown here in Chapter 10.) The other items on the left side of the Start menu reflect the programs you've most recently used. You can choose to display more or fewer items, as you'll see in Chapter 10.

Note   The process of pointing to an item and then clicking the mouse's left button is called clicking the item, and I'll refer to it as such in the pages that follow.

The items on the right side of the Start menu also depend, to some extent, on how your computer is set up. For example, if your computer is not on a network, you won't see the My Network Places or Connect To items. Here's a description of what happens when you click the other items on the Start menu:

- Clicking My Documents opens your My Documents folder (discussed in Chapter 3).
- Clicking My Recent Documents displays a list of the last 15 documents you opened.
- Clicking My Pictures opens your My Pictures folder (discussed in Chapter 3).
- Clicking My Music opens your My Music folder (discussed in Chapter 3).
- Clicking My Computer opens the My Computer folder, which is a window onto the files and devices on your computer.
- Clicking Control Panel opens Control Panel, which you use to configure and/or customize Windows XP. (Chapter 10 discusses Control Panel in detail).

- Clicking Printers and Faxes opens the Printers and Faxes folder (discussed in Chapter 4).
- Clicking Help and Support opens the Windows XP Help and Support Center, a much improved version of Windows Help. (Chapter 9 discusses Help and Support Center.)
- Clicking Search starts the Search Companion, which you can use to search your computer or the Internet.
- Clicking Run opens the Run dialog box, which you can use to enter a command to start a program, open a file, connect to an Internet resource, and so on.

The remaining item on the Start menu is All Programs. When you point to All Programs, Windows lists the programs you can start (see Figure 1-5). This list displays programs that are included with Windows XP as well as any other programs you have installed on your system. I'll discuss the Windows XP programs in later chapters in this book.

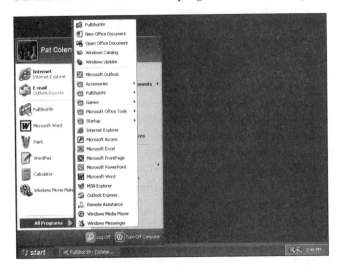

FIGURE 1-5

The Windows desktop showing the All Programs menu.

If you or someone else did a clean install of Windows XP on your system, you may see only one shortcut icon on the desktop, the Recycle Bin. On the other hand, if you bought a new computer on which Windows XP was already installed, you might see several shortcut icons. Shortcut icons are clickable pictures you can use to start a program, open a document or folder, or use in a variety of other ways that I'll discuss later in this chapter and in those that follow.

Note The process of clicking an item quickly twice in a row is called **double-clicking** the item, and I'll refer to it as such in the pages that follow.

If you double-click the Recycle Bin icon, you open the Recycle Bin folder, which is a special container Windows uses to temporarily store the files you've deleted. Figure 1-6 shows the

Recycle Bin folder in its own window. (A window is just a rectangle that Windows uses to display information.)

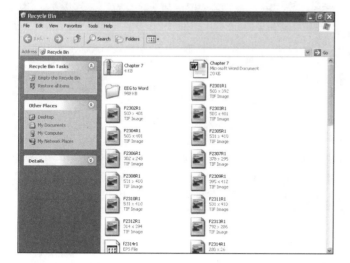

FIGURE 1-6

The Recycle Bin folder temporarily stores the files you've deleted.

If you're using your computer to follow along with this chapter's discussion, double-click the Recycle Bin icon to see how shortcut icons work. If you or someone else has recently deleted any files, you will see them listed here. When you want to remove the window showing the Recycle Bin from your desktop, click the Close button, the small "X" button that appears in the upper-right corner of the window.

Note   Chapter 3, "Files, Folders, and Disks," talks in detail about how and why you delete files—and why you might want to undelete them.

The Taskbar is the third key element of the Windows desktop (see Figure 1-3). After you start a program, Windows adds a program button to the Taskbar. Whenever you want to use the program, you click its button. This sounds confusing, perhaps. But rather than go into more detail here, let me move on to a discussion of how you start and stop programs. Once you know how to do this, I can show you how the Taskbar and program buttons work.

At the far right of the Taskbar is the notification area, which by default, usually displays only the time. If you hover the mouse cursor over the time, the current date is displayed. You may also see icons for other currently running services on your system. If your computer is connected to a local area network, you may see a little computer that indicates the network is up and running, and when you connect to the Internet, you may see another computer icon for that connection. If you hover the mouse over either of these icons, you'll see a description that shows the speed and other aspects of the connection. Chapter 10 discusses how to customize the notification area.

Starting Windows Programs

With what you now know, you can easily start Windows programs. Let's say, for example, that you want to start the Windows Calculator program. To do so, follow these steps:

1 Start Windows if necessary.

2 Click the Start button.

3 Point to All Programs, and point to Accessories.

4 Click Calculator.

Note Finding a program takes a bit of work sometimes. Some programs, such as the Windows Help program (which I'll talk about in Chapter 9, "Troubleshooting Windows XP"), appear on the Start menu. Other programs appear on the All Programs menu. Much of the time, however, choosing an item from the All Programs menu displays a submenu, and this is where the program you want will appear. This is the case with the Calculator program.

When you click Calculator on the Accessories menu, Windows starts the Calculator program, as shown in Figure 1-7. Notice that Windows opens a new window for the Calculator program. Windows also adds an item on the Start menu for the Calculator program.

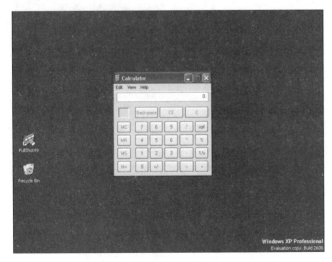

FIGURE 1-7

The Calculator program window on top of the Windows desktop.

You can start, or "run," more than one program at a time with Windows, which is known as multitasking. In fact, you can even start the same program twice. For example, if you were working on two separate calculations, you could start the Calculator program twice, and in this case, you would actually have two Calculator programs running. Windows would open program windows for both programs, and Windows would also add program buttons on the Taskbar for both programs (see Figure 1-8).

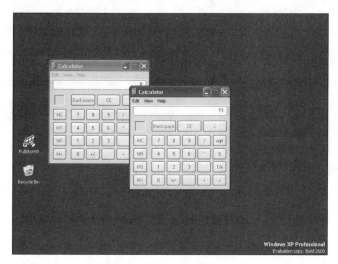

FIGURE 1-8

This Windows desktop shows two Calculator program windows. The active Calculator is the top window.

When you multitask, one of the programs you've started is the active program. The active program's window appears on top of any other windows if they overlap. When you issue a command, Windows assumes that you're issuing the command to the active program. (I'll talk about issuing commands in the next chapter.) If you want to see another program's window or make another program active—perhaps so that you can issue a command—you click its program button on the Taskbar.

Let me make one final comment about multitasking. Although multitasking sounds complicated, you'll want to do this. Multitasking is akin to using more than one tool at a time. On your desk, for example—the one you're perhaps sitting at right now—you probably have pencils, a stapler, scissors, and so on. Having these tools on your desktop, within reach, makes it easier to use them. You don't need to put away one tool every time you start a new task or project. Multitasking with Windows works the same way. By multitasking, you don't have to stop what you're doing every time you temporarily stop using a particular tool. You keep several programs ready and waiting to use when you need them.

Stopping Windows Programs

You stop, or "exit" or "quit," Windows programs after you're finished using them. You can do this in three ways: by using the program window's Close button, by using a menu command in the program, and as a last resort method, by telling Windows to close a program. I'll describe all the methods because you'll have occasion to use all three.

Using the Close Button to Stop a Program

Let's start with the easiest way to stop a Windows program. You can remove any window from the Windows desktop by clicking the small "X" in the box—called the Close button—that appears in the upper-right corner of the window. If you close a program window, you stop the program. When you stop the program, Windows removes the window from the Windows desktop and the program button from the Taskbar. (If you're following along on your computer with this chapter's discussion and have two Calculator program windows on your desktop, go ahead and close one of them this way.)

Using the File Menu's Exit Command

Most programs also provide a command you can use to stop them. To see how this works, start the WordPad accessory program by clicking the Start button, pointing to All Programs and then Accessories, and then clicking WordPad. When Windows displays the WordPad program window (see Figure 1-9), click the word *File* that is found just below the upper-left corner of the program window so that the File menu appears, and then click the Exit command. This process—choosing the File menu's Exit command—stops the program.

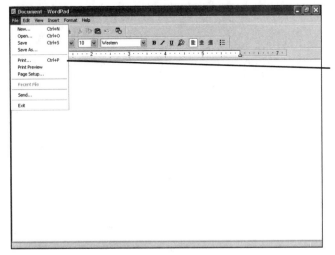

FIGURE 1-9

The WordPad program window with the File menu activated.

The File menu.

Note Chapter 2, "Windows, Commands, and Dialog Boxes," talks in greater detail about how you choose commands, including the File menu's Exit command.

Using Task Manager to Close a Program

Sometimes the Close button and the File menu's Exit command don't work. Sometimes—not often, but still too frequently—a program stops responding to commands. Unfortunately, in this case, you can't tell the program to stop. In this case, you have to tell Windows to stop the program. To tell Windows to stop a program, follow these steps:

1 Press the Ctrl, Alt, and Delete keys simultaneously. Windows opens the Windows Task Manager dialog box, which displays a list of the programs you've started (see Figure 1-10).

FIGURE 1-10

Using the Task Manager to close a program.

2 In the Task list on the Applications tab, click the program that won't close in one of the usual ways. Note that Windows probably identifies the program as "Not responding."

3 Click the End Task button.

4 Click the OK button when Windows asks you to confirm that you want to close the unresponsive program.

Stopping Windows XP

When you finish working with your computer, you want to stop Windows before you turn off your computer. You can do this in one of two ways. The typical way to stop Windows is by using the Turn Off Computer command. To do this, follow these steps:

1 Click the Start button.

2 Click the Turn Off Computer button to display the Turn Off Computer dialog box (see Figure 1-11).

3 Click the Turn Off button.

FIGURE 1-11

Turning off the computer.

You'll also notice two other buttons in the Turn Off Computer dialog box: Hibernate (if your computer supports hibernation) and Restart. Clicking Hibernate writes all the data in memory to a hibernation file on the hard drive. During hibernation, all your programs and documents are open so when the computer emerges from hibernation you can start working right where you left off. Clicking Restart powers down your computer and then turns it back on without your intervention.

You can also shut down your computer in the following ways:

- Click the Turn Off button on the Welcome screen and then click the Turn Off button in the Turn Off Computer dialog box.
- In Windows Task Manager, click Shut Down, and then click Turn Off.
- From the desktop, press Alt+F4 to open the Turn Off Computer dialog box, and then click Turn Off.

Although Windows XP is arguably the most stable version of Windows ever, the inevitable crash will occur. If you aren't able to display the Turn Off Computer dialog box, you'll need to stop Windows by pressing the power button on the computer. If a short press doesn't do the job, as is the case with one of my computers, press and hold the power button for about four or more seconds. On some computers, a quick press of the power button will display the Turn Off Computer dialog box. In this case, you can then stop Windows in the normal way.

Chapter 2

Windows, Commands, and Dialog Boxes

Before you can begin using Microsoft Windows XP productively and comfortably, you need to know how to communicate with Windows by using its interface. Fortunately, learning to work with the Windows interface is very easy. But you will need to learn how to do several things. This chapter provides this information by talking about:

- Using Windows' windows
- Issuing commands
- Using dialog boxes

Using Windows' Windows

Microsoft named the Windows operating system "Windows" because it displays information by using windows. A window is the rectangle that the Windows operating system or any other program uses to enclose the information on your screen. For example, in Figure 2-1, you can see that on top of the Windows desktop, the Calculator program appears as a rectangle: this is the Calculator program window. Underneath the Calculator program window, you see another program window: this is the WordPad program window.

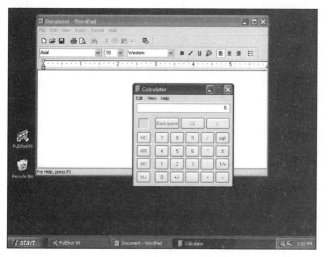

FIGURE 2-1

The Calculator program window and the WordPad program window are displayed on top of the Windows desktop.

Moving Windows

You can move a window or a dialog box by dragging its title bar. To drag a title bar or any other item, click the item and then, while continuing to hold down the left mouse button, move the mouse. The title bar is the colored bar that appears along the top edge of the window.

You can also select or drag an item without holding down the mouse button continuously if the ClickLock feature is enabled. Simply press and hold down a mouse button or a trackball button for a moment. You can then drag objects or make multiple selections. When the operation is complete, click the mouse or trackball button again to release ClickLock. You'll probably want to experiment to see if you prefer to use ClickLock.

To enable or disable ClickLock, follow these steps:

1 Click Start, and then click Control Panel to open the Control Panel.

2 Click the Printers And Other Hardware link, and then click Mouse to open the Mouse Properties dialog box, which is shown in Figure 2-2.

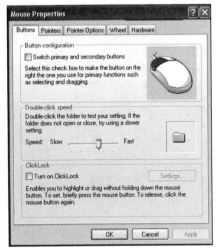

FIGURE 2-2

The Mouse Properties dialog box, open at the Buttons tab.

3 Click the Buttons tab.

4 Click the Turn On ClickLock check box to enable ClickLock. If the check box is selected (checked), click to clear it.

5 Click OK.

2

Stacking and Restacking Windows

You can easily stack and restack the windows that appear on your Windows desktop:

- To move a window to the top of a stack of windows, click it.
- To move a window to the top of your desktop from the Taskbar, click the program's or document's button on the Taskbar.

Figure 2-3 shows a stack of windows on the desktop. The Outlook Express window is the active window, the window that appears on the top of the stack. Windows assumes that when you issue a command, you're issuing the command to the active window. Windows also assumes that when you type in some bit of information, you want that information placed in the active window. When you close the active window, Windows automatically makes the window under the just-closed window the new active window.

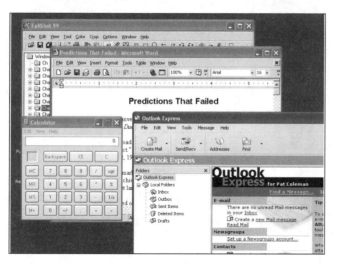

FIGURE 2-3

The window at the top of the stack is the active window.

Note As mentioned in Chapter 1, you close a window by clicking its Close button. The Close button is the small box marked with an "X" that appears in the upper-right corner of every program window and every document window.

Resizing Windows

Windows provides easy-to-use resizing buttons so that you can change the size of windows or even hide windows. Windows also provides a resizing box so that you can adjust a window to the size of your choice.

You can tell Windows to enlarge a window so that it fills the desktop. To do this, click the Maximize button. The Maximize button appears to the left of the Close button (as long as a window isn't already maximized). Figure 2-4 shows a regular size Microsoft Word program window. If you clicked the Maximize button in both of these windows, Windows would maximize the windows so that they looked like those shown in Figure 2-5.

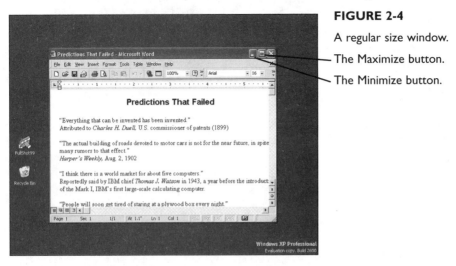

FIGURE 2-4

A regular size window.

The Maximize button.

The Minimize button.

Note If you're working in one program on one document, you typically want to work with maximized windows to make them as big and easy to view as possible. If you're working with multiple programs and documents, you typically want to work with regular-size windows so that you can restack the windows with a simple mouse click.

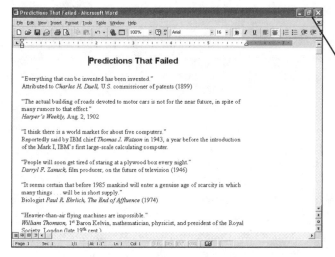

FIGURE 2-5

A maximized Microsoft Word window.

The Restore button.

After you maximize a window, Windows replaces the Maximize button with the Restore button. To restore a maximized window to its original size, click the Restore button. You can also minimize windows. When you minimize a window, the window no longer appears on the desktop but its program button still appears on the Taskbar. You can restore a minimized window by clicking its button on the Taskbar.

Windows also provides one other handy tool for resizing windows. As long as a window isn't maximized or minimized, Windows adds a Resizing box to the lower-right corner (see Figure 2-6). You can resize a window by dragging this box up or down and to the right or left. Note that the pointer turns into a double-headed arrow when you point to the Resizing box.

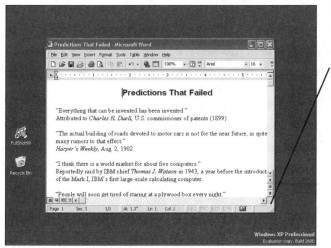

FIGURE 2-6

Use the Resizing box to change program window and document window size.

The Resizing box.

Issuing Commands

Once you're comfortable working with Windows' windows, you'll want to learn how to issue commands to Windows and to Windows programs. Typically, you issue commands from within a program in one of three ways: by choosing menu bar commands, by clicking toolbar buttons, and by choosing shortcut menu commands. You'll want to know how each of these techniques works because at various times you'll find you need to use all three.

Before I get into these three ways to issue commands from within a program, though, I need to point out that Windows XP provides a number of keyboard combinations for issuing commands to Windows itself. These combinations involve pressing the Winkey (pronounced Win-key, not winky), the key on the keyboard that has the Windows logo on it, while pressing another key or keys. If you're comfortable at the keyboard, you'll find using a Winkey combination much faster in many cases than reaching for the mouse. Table 2-1 lists the Winkey combinations. Don't worry if you see unfamiliar items in the What It Does column. You'll encounter an explanation of all these items in future chapters.

Winkey Combination	**What It Does**
Winkey	Toggles (turns on and off) the display of the Start menu
Winkey+Break	Displays the System Properties dialog box
Winkey+Tab	Moves the focus to the next button in the Taskbar
Winkey+Shift+Tab	Moves the focus to the previous button in the Taskbar
Winkey+B	Moves the focus to the notification area
Winkey+D	Displays the desktop
Winkey+E	Opens an Explorer window showing My Computer
Winkey+F	Opens a Search Results window and activates Search Companion
Winkey+Ctrl+F	Opens a Search Results window, activates Search Companion, and starts a Search for Computer
Winkey+F1	Opens a Help and Support Center window
Winkey+M	Issues a Minimize All command
Winkey+Shift+M	Issues an Undo Minimize All command
Winkey+R	Displays the Run dialog box
Winkey+U	Displays Utility Manager
Winkey+L	Locks the computer

Table 2-1: Winkey combinations in Windows XP.

	If you've been following along on your computer with the discussion in this chapter or the previous one, you've already issued a command or two to Windows or to a Windows program. You can't really do anything with either Windows or one of its programs except by issuing a command. You start and stop programs by issuing commands, as described in Chapter 1.
Note	

	If you want to follow along on your computer with the discussion here, go ahead and start the WordPad program. To do this, click the Start button, point to All Programs and then Accessories, and then click WordPad.
Note	

Using Menu Bar Commands

The first way to issue commands in a program is by using menu bars. Most programs display a row of menu names directly beneath the title bar. If you look at the WordPad program window shown in Figure 2-7, you see the words *File, Edit, View, Insert, Format,* and *Help.* These words constitute the menu bar.

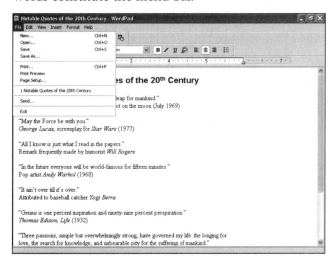

FIGURE 2-7

The WordPad program window with the File menu activated.

If you click on a menu bar item—the word *File,* for example—the program activates the menu so that its choices are displayed. After you activate a menu, you can then choose any of its commands by clicking. For example, in Figure 2-7, you can choose the File menu's New command by clicking on the first menu item, the one that is labeled New.

| Note | Don't worry about the functions of the various commands at this point. I'll discuss many commands in the chapters that follow. |

Using a mouse is the easiest way to issue commands in Windows, but you can also use the keyboard in the following two ways:

- Press the Alt key to activate the menu bar and display the underlined letter in the menu and the command name, and then choose a menu and a command by typing the underlined letter in the menu and the command name. For example, you can select the File menu's New command by pressing Alt, F, and then N.

- Press a key combination for a command if the command provides one. For example, in Figure 2-7, across from the New command name is the text *Ctrl+N*. This information tells you that pressing the N key while pressing the Ctrl key chooses the File menu's New command.

Once you choose a command, Windows (or the program you're issuing the command to) either executes the command or displays a dialog box to collect more information before executing the command.

| Note | If a command collects more information by using a dialog box, the command name is followed by an ellipsis ("..."). |

Because all of a program's commands are available through its menu bar menus, you'll often have dozens and dozens of commands to sift through. Programs organize commands into categories by using the menu bar menu—File, Edit, View, and so on—but sometimes that's not enough. Some of the items on menu bar menus aren't commands, they're actually submenus. If selected, these submenus display additional commands. Menu items that represent submenus are followed by arrows. In Figure 2-8, for example, the View menu's Toolbars item is followed by an arrow, which tells you that the Toolbars item has a submenu.

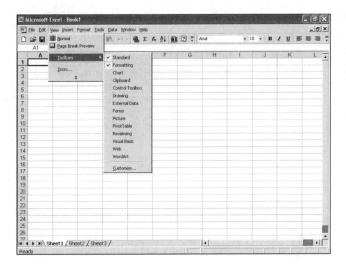

FIGURE 2-8

Powerful programs, such as Microsoft Excel, often use both menus and submenus to organize their numerous commands.

2

Note Microsoft Excel is a spreadsheet program used for the numerical analysis involved in developing budgets or making financial forecasts.

Using Toolbar Buttons

The second way to issue commands is by using toolbars. A toolbar provides clickable buttons to use in place of menu bar commands (see Figure 2-9). In WordPad, for example, if you click the Standard toolbar's fourth button (counting from the left), you issue the File menu's Print command, and WordPad prints the document.

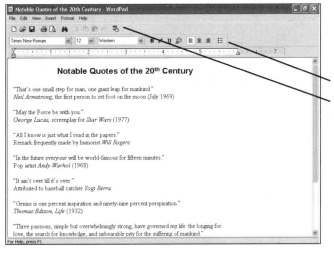

FIGURE 2-9

The WordPad program, like many programs, provides toolbars with buttons you can click to issue commands.

The Formatting toolbar.

The Standard toolbar.

Toolbar button pictures, or icons, identify the function of the toolbar button. In WordPad, for example, the Print button shows a picture of a printer. In addition, if you point to a toolbar button with the mouse, a little yellow window pops up with the button's name in it. If you point to the Print button, for example, Windows displays a pop-up window with the name "Print."

Because toolbar buttons make it easier to issue common commands, they can work really well for new users. And, in fact, in the pages that follow, I'll emphasize toolbar buttons when available.

Note   If you want to experiment with toolbar buttons, start WordPad and then type some text into the window. Next, double-click a word and then click a toolbar button on the Format Bar. Then double-click another word and click another toolbar button on the Format Bar. When you're finished, click the Close button to stop the program. When WordPad asks if you want to save your document, click the No button.

Using Shortcut Menu Commands

The third way to issue commands is by using shortcut menus. Shortcut menus give you a list of those commands that are appropriate for working with a particular object or item. Let me show you how this works.

Suppose that you're using WordPad to create the document shown in Figure 2-10, and in this document you want to do something with the word *small*. Perhaps you want to format it in some way, but you don't know which menu bar command to use and you can't figure out which toolbar button is appropriate. If you right-click the word, the WordPad program, with the help of Windows, displays a shortcut menu of commands you can use.

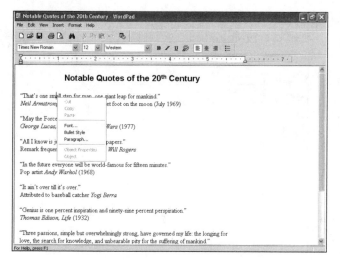

FIGURE 2-10

Right-click to display shortcut menus such as this one. "Right-click" means to click with the right mouse button instead of the left mouse button.

2

Note If you've switched the mouse-button functions, say because you are left-handed, you'll need to left-click to display a shortcut menu.

Note Because shortcut menu commands are so useful, I'll emphasize this command choice method whenever possible.

Using Dialog Boxes

Sometimes, when you issue a command, Windows or a program needs more information. When this is the case, Windows displays a dialog box to collect the information it, or the program, needs. For example, if you're working with the WordPad program and you choose the File menu's Print command, WordPad displays the Print dialog box. As Figure 2-11 shows (next page), dialog boxes provide a variety of buttons and boxes. You use these buttons and boxes to describe how Windows or a program should carry out a command.

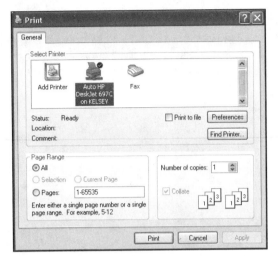

FIGURE 2-11

The Print dialog box.

Command Buttons

You typically use command buttons to tell Windows or a program what it should do with the information you've provided using a dialog box. For example, almost every dialog box provides an OK and a Cancel button. Sometimes, though, a more specifically named button may replace the OK button. For example, the Print dialog box in Figure 2-11 has a Print button instead of an OK button. You click the OK command button (or press the Enter key) to indicate that Windows or the program should use the dialog box information to complete the command you've issued. You click the Cancel command button (or press Esc on the keyboard) to tell Windows or the program that it shouldn't do anything with the dialog box information and, in fact, that you want to cancel your command. Sometimes you'll also see other command buttons in a dialog box. Figure 2-11, for example, provides a Preferences command button. Clicking this Preferences command button displays another dialog box that lets you tell Windows how your printer should work.

Let me make one other comment about command buttons. One of the command buttons in a dialog box is always active, and you can tell which one it is by the thick border drawn around it. In Figure 2-11, for example, the Print button is active. You can select the active command button by clicking it with the mouse or by pressing the Enter key.

Note Very simple dialog boxes that use only command buttons are sometimes known as message boxes.

The Question Mark Button

In the upper-right corner of most dialog boxes, next to the Close button, is the Question Mark button. Click the Question Mark button and then click an option in the dialog box to display an explanation of the option in a pop-up window. In Figure 2-12, for example, Windows displays this pop-up window when you click the Print button. Click outside the pop-up window to close it.

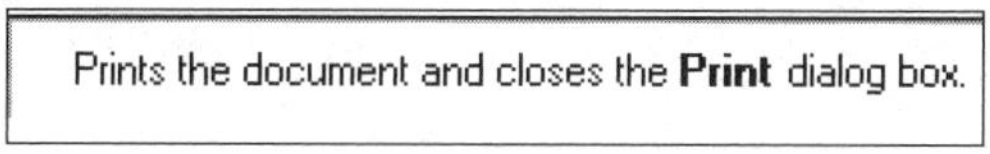

> Prints the document and closes the **Print** dialog box.

FIGURE 2-12

The pop-up window that describes the Print button.

List Boxes

List boxes display choices you can select. In Figure 2-13, for example, the Paper Source list box lists the paper sources you can use to print a WordPad document. (The Paper Source list box is actually a special kind of space-conserving list box called a drop-down list box. To select an entry from a drop-down list box, click the down arrow button that appears at the right end of the list. When you do this, Windows activates, or drops down, the list.) You select a list box entry by clicking it. Figure 2-13 shows the dropped-down Paper Source list box.

FIGURE 2-13

The dropped-down Paper Source list box.

Note   Chapter 4, "Printing," describes how you print with Windows and how you install printers for use with Windows and Windows programs.

Clicking is the easiest way to activate a list box and select an entry, but you can also use the keyboard. To select a list box, press the Alt key to display the underlined letter in the list box name, and then press Alt and the underlined letter in the list box name. (For example, you press Alt+S to select the Paper Source list box.) To drop-down the Paper Source list box, press the Alt key and then the down arrow key. Once Windows drops down, or activates, the list box, use the up and down arrow keys to highlight the list entry you want. Press the Enter key to close the list box, or press the Tab key to close the list box and move to another dialog box element.

If you prefer using the keyboard to using the mouse, you can tell Windows to always display the underlined letters in menus and dialog boxes. Right-click an empty area of the desktop, and choose Properties from the shortcut menu to display the Display Properties dialog box. Click the Appearance tab, and then click the Effects button to open the Effects dialog box. Clear the Hide Underlined Letters For Keyboard Navigation Until I Press The Alt Key check box, and then click OK. Click OK again to close the Display Properties dialog box.

Note   You can also select a dialog box button or box by pressing the Tab key until the button or box is highlighted.

Option Buttons

Option buttons present lists of mutually exclusive choices. The Print dialog box shown in Figure 2-11, for example, includes Page Range option buttons: All, Selection, Current Page, and Pages. By clicking an option button, you describe which pages you want to print: click All to print all the pages in the WordPad document, click Selection to print the selected portion of the WordPad document, click Current Page to print the page in which the insertion point currently resides, and click Pages and then specify the range to print only a range of pages. (You select a portion of a WordPad document by clicking the mouse at the beginning of the text you want, holding the left button down, moving the mouse to the end of the text, and releasing the button. Windows will highlight the text.)

To select an option button with the mouse, click the button. To select an option button using the keyboard, press the Alt key to display the underlined letter in the option button name, and then press Alt and the underlined letter. To select the All button, for example, press Alt+L.

Check Boxes

Check boxes work like on-off switches. For example, the Print To File check box shown in Figure 2-11 is an on-off switch that tells Windows to print to a file rather than to the printer. If you want to print to a file, check the box by clicking it. You can also check or clear a box by pressing the Alt key to display the underlined letter in the check box name, and then press Alt and the underlined letter in the check box name. For example, to check or clear the Print To File check box, press Alt+F.

Note As a practical matter, you won't need to print to a file. Typically, the only people who print to files are desktop publishers creating books and newsletters.

Text Boxes

Text boxes are blank boxes that you fill in by typing. In Figure 2-11, for example, to the right of the Pages option button is a text box in which you can enter the numbered range of the pages you want to print. After you click the Pages option button, you then fill in this box.

To use a text box, select it and then type a number or some text in the box. You can select a text box by clicking or by pressing the Alt key and the underlined letter in the text box name. (If the underlined letters are not displayed, press Alt and then press the Alt key combination.) To print from page 4 to page 12, for example, follow these steps:

1 Click the text box next to the Pages option button.

2 Type 4-12.

You can edit the information you enter in a text box in the following ways:

- To replace the entire contents of a text box, you can sometimes click the text box to select the text box contents. To replace the highlighted contents, just type the new text.

- To change some portion of the text box contents, select the text you want to replace by clicking the first character you want to type and dragging the mouse to the last character you want to replace. After you've highlighted the text you want to replace, type the new text.

- To insert text in existing text, click at the exact point where you want to insert the new text. Then type your text.

- To erase text, click to the right of the last character you want to delete and then press the Backspace key as many times as characters you want to erase. Alternatively, click to the left of the first character you want to delete and then press the Delete key as many times as characters you want to erase.

Let me make a couple more comments about text boxes. First, along with the blank that can be filled in, some text boxes also include a drop-down list of selections. Second, some text boxes that accept numeric values include up and down arrow buttons so that you can add or subtract 1 from the value displayed in the text box. In Figure 2-11, for example, clicking the up arrow button in the Number Of Copies text box adds 1 to the displayed value and clicking the down arrow button subtracts 1 from the displayed value.

Sliders

You use sliders to make incremental adjustments, such as changes for volume or speed. Figure 2-14 shows a slider.

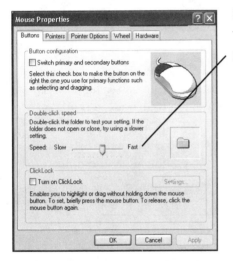

FIGURE 2-14

The Mouse Properties dialog box includes a slider.

Drag this slider to change your mouse's double-click speed.

Note To follow along with this discussion on your computer, click the Start button, click Control Panel, click the Printers and Other Hardware link, and then click the Mouse link. Chapter 10, "Customizing Windows XP," describes in detail how you use Control Panel tools to change the way Windows works.

To use a slider, drag it with the mouse. In Figure 2-14, for example, dragging the slider to the left reduces the mouse's double-click speed. Dragging the slider to the right increases the mouse's double-click speed.

Tabs

Figure 2-14 illustrates one other dialog box element, tabs. Because there isn't room to display all the Mouse Properties buttons and boxes at the same time, Windows segregates them on different pages: Buttons, Pointers, Pointer Options, Wheel, and Hardware. To see another page, just click its tab.

You now know enough to get you started so that you can work with the buttons and boxes that appear in the dialog boxes you'll encounter. Note, however, that while dialog box buttons and boxes work in the ways I've described here, they don't always look identical to the buttons and boxes shown here. Command buttons might have pictures on their faces, for example, or even look like a picture or some object. A check box might be round rather than square. An option button might be square instead of round, and so on. So don't let appearances throw you.

Chapter 3

Files, Folders, and Disks

Once you know how to start Microsoft Windows XP and Windows programs and how to work with commands, dialog boxes, and windows, you'll want to learn how to manage files, folders, and disks. This chapter helps you acquire this critically important knowledge by discussing three important topics:

- Defining the key terms
- Working with files, folders, and disks
- Performing housekeeping tasks

Defining the Key Terms

Before you can understand how you use Windows to work with the information that you collect and store on your computer, you need to understand four terms: file, folder, disk, and document. So let's do that here.

A file is the information that Windows stores. If you type a letter to your mother, for example, Windows stores your letter as a file. If you use an illustration program such as Microsoft Paint to create a picture, Windows stores your picture as a file.

Note Chapter 7, "Windows XP Accessories," describes how you use the Microsoft Paint program, as well as several other Windows accessory programs.

Once you know what a file is, everything else falls into place. A folder is the container used to store a set of files. Typically you use folders to group files. For example, you might use one folder to hold all documents related to a certain project. And you might use another folder to hold all your contracts.

A disk is the physical storage device your computer uses to store your files. Your computer probably has a hard disk, sometimes called a hard drive, and that's just a stack of metal platters in your computer. Your computer probably also has a CD-ROM drive, which you use to read files from compact disks, or CDs. And if you bought your computer recently, it probably also has a DVD drive. And some computers also have other, more exotic types of storage disks.

To summarize, a file stores the information you collect using your computer. A folder is the container you use to group, or organize, your files. And a disk is the physical storage unit where files and folders are located. Here's a metaphor to help you understand the structure. Think of a disk as being like a filing cabinet. The folders are like the cabinet drawers, and your computer files are like the paper files stored inside the filing cabinet drawers.

Now that you know what files, folders, and disks are, let me make two more points. First, files fall into two categories: document files and program files. The files that you create—a letter, a picture, or a report, for example—are document files, or documents. But if you start rummaging around in your computer's folders, you're going to see files you didn't create. These are program files. Program files store the software instructions that a software program (like your word processor) uses to function.

Here's the second point. Practically speaking, you name your folders and files—and you can name them whatever you want. Okay, in truth, some rules do apply, but they are very loose. If you unintentionally break a rule, nothing bad happens. Windows just says, "Oh, you can't use that name because it violates this rule…" Windows, however, names its disks using the letters of the alphabet. Your floppy disk is probably named A. Your hard disk is probably named C. And your CD-ROM drive is probably named D. If your computer has other disks, Windows uses other letters—E, F, G, and so on—for their names.

Working with Files, Folders, and Disks

Once you understand what files, folders, and disks are, you're ready to begin working with them. You can work with these items in a variety of ways, but the easiest way is by using the My Computer folder.

Reviewing the My Computer Folder

To open the My Computer folder, click Start, and then click My Computer. Figure 3-1 shows the My Computer folder on one of my computers.

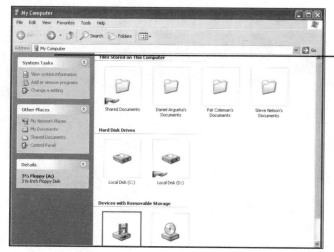

FIGURE 3-1

The My Computer folder.

Explorer Bar.

At the top of the My Computer folder is a title bar. Beneath that is a menu bar, and beneath the menu bar is a toolbar. (I'll be describing some of the menu bar commands and toolbar buttons in the coming paragraphs, but as promised in Chapter 2, I'll be emphasizing shortcut menu commands because they're faster and easier to use.) Initially, the My Computer folder shows icons representing the files stored on your computer and the disks your computer uses. On the left side is an Explorer Bar that contains links you can click to display other folders or perform certain tasks.

You have two ways of viewing the My Computer folder. If you click the Folders button on the toolbar, you'll see the view shown in Figure 3-2 (next page). In this case the Explorer bar has been replaced with the Folders bar, a hierarchical list of the drives and folders on your computer system. Click the plus sign next to an item to expand it and display the items that are stored within it. Click a minus sign next to an item to contract the list beneath that item. When you expand an item, its contents are displayed in the pane on the right.

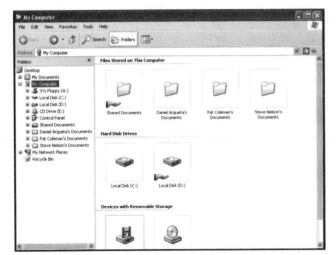

FIGURE 3-2

Another view of the My Computer folder.

You can further view the My Computer folder in several other ways. The view shown in both Figure 3-1 and Figure 3-2 is called Thumbnails, small pictorial representations of folders and disks. Your other view choices are Tile, Icons, List, and Details, and if the items in a selected folder are pictures, you'll see the My Computer folder in Filmstrip view. To select a view, you use the View menu. Check out the various views by clicking the File menu and then clicking one of the views. The view you choose depends on the task at hand and, of course, your personal preference. Later in this chapter I'll discuss the My Pictures folder, but for now, to get an idea of how changing the view works, let's look at the Filmstrip view of a My Pictures folder, as shown in Figure 3-3. In the Folders bar, click the icon for your documents to expand the folder, and then click the My Pictures folder. Double-click the Sample Pictures folder, and you'll see something similar to Figure 3-3 if you haven't added your own picture files to this folder.

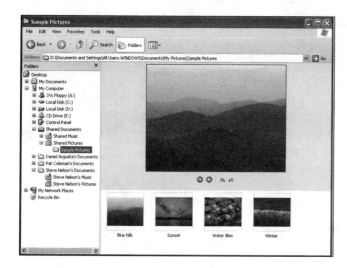

FIGURE 3-3

The My Pictures folder in Filmstrip view.

Select a thumbnail at the bottom of the screen to display it in an enlarged view above. You use the buttons just below the enlargement as follows (from left to right):

- Click Previous Image to view the picture you were looking at before.
- Click Next Image to view the next picture in the row of thumbnails.
- Click Rotate Clockwise to turn the picture 90 degrees to the right.
- Click Rotate Counterclockwise to turn the picture 90 degrees to the left.

Later in this chapter, I'll describe how you can use your My Pictures folder in some specific ways.

Folders That Windows XP Sets Up

As you know from Chapter 1, Windows XP is a multi-user computer environment, and for each user who has an account on your system, Windows XP sets up a My Documents folder. Figures 3-1 and 3-2 show the My Documents folder for the users on my computer. As you can see, your My Documents folder will display your name and then the word "Folder." Windows suggests that your My Documents folder is the logical place to store the documents that you create. (Later in this chapter, I'll discuss how you do this.) But inside each My Documents folder are other folders. At the very least, you'll have a My Pictures folder and a My Music folder. By default when you download photos from a digital camera to your computer or when you scan them in, Windows XP stores them in the My Pictures folder and dates them. When you copy music from your CD-ROM drive to your computer or download music from the Internet, Windows XP automatically stores those files in your My Music folder.

You'll have some additional folders in your My Documents folder if you have installed the Fax Service (see Chapter 7), if you have accessed video files, and so on.

Windows XP also sets up a Shared Documents folder. Any documents in this folder are available to all users of your computer.

If you want more information about a file that appears in the My Computer folder, right-click it (either in the Explorer Bar or in the pane on the right), and choose Properties from the shortcut menu. Windows displays a dialog box that describes the file's properties (see Figure 3-4). In Figure 3-4, for example, the dialog box names the file, gives its folder location, and reports on its size in bytes and kilobytes. (A kilobyte, by the way, is roughly 1,000 bytes.) The Properties dialog box also reports other information about the file, such as the date the file was created, last modified, and most recently accessed, and the file's attributes: whether the file is typically hidden from view when the My Computer folder is open, whether the file is read-only (which means you can look at the file but you can't change it), and so on.

FIGURE 3-4

The Properties dialog box describes a file in more detail.

Note   If you have Windows XP Home Edition installed on your computer, you won't see the Security tab shown in the Properties dialog box in Figure 3-4. If you have Windows XP Professional installed on your computer and don't see the Security tab, you can display it. Click the Start button, and then click Control Panel to open Control Panel. Click the Appearances And Themes link, and then click the Folder Options link. In the Folder Options dialog box, click the View tab, and in the Advanced Settings list, clear the Use Simple File Sharing (Recommended) check box.

Opening Documents

You can open a document in two ways with Windows. You can tell Windows that you want to work with a document. Windows then looks at the document, figures out which program it needs to work with the document, starts that program, and tells that program to grab the document and display it. You can also open a document by first starting the program you'll use to work with the document, and then telling this program to open the document.

To open a document using Windows, open the My Computer folder and then follow these steps:

1 Open your My Documents folder if it contains the file or folder you want to open by double-clicking it.

2 If the document is in a subfolder, double-click the subfolder to open it and display its files.

3 Open the document by double-clicking the document.

To open a document using a program rather than using Windows, follow these steps:

1 Start the program you'll use to work with the document as described in Chapter 1.

2 Choose the File menu's Open command. The program displays the Open dialog box (see Figure 3-5).

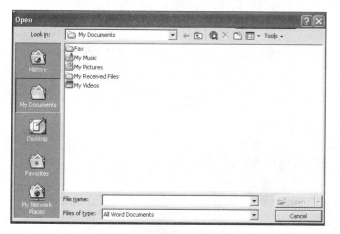

FIGURE 3-5

The Open dialog box.

3 Use the Look In drop-down list box to identify the disk and folder containing the file you want to open. To see the files inside a folder, double-click the folder.

4 When you see the document file listed in the box beneath the Look In drop-down list box, open it by double-clicking it.

Windows typically creates a special folder called My Documents and assumes that you'll use this folder to store the documents you create. For this reason, you'll notice that the Open dialog box initially shows the files in the My Documents folder.

Saving Documents

You save a document with the program used to create the document. For example, if you're using your word processor to write a friend a letter, you use the word processor to save the letter. To save a document within a program, follow these steps:

1 Choose the File menu's Save As command. The program displays a Save As dialog box such as the one shown in Figure 3-6.

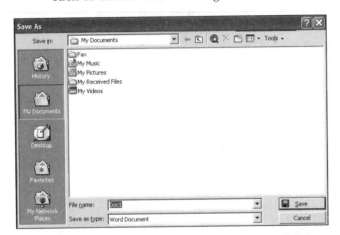

FIGURE 3-6

The Save As dialog box.

2 Use the Save In drop-down list box to identify the disk and folder in which you want to store the file. Again, to see the files inside a folder, just double-click the folder.

3 Type a name for the document file in the File Name box.

Note Each file in a folder must have a unique name, and each subfolder in a folder must have a unique name. For example, you could have a file named January Report in the Annual Report folder, and you could have a file named January Report in the Management Memos folder, but you cannot have two files both named January Report in the Annual Report folder.

---

4 Click the Save button.

Note To save changes to a document file you've already saved, choose the File menu's Save command or click the Save toolbar button if one is provided.

Renaming Documents

You can easily rename a document file. First, open the My Computer folder and then find the disk and folder you want. You do this as described in the earlier section "Reviewing the My Computer Folder." Once you find the file, you can rename it in any of three ways:

- Right-click the file name and from the shortcut menu choose Rename. Windows places a box around the document name and highlights the current name (see Figure 3-7). Type the new document name you want, and then click outside the box.

- Click the file name once to select it and then, after a brief pause, click it again or press the keyboard key labeled F2. Windows places a box around the document name and highlights the current name. Type the new document name you want, and then click outside the box.

- If the My Computer folder displays the Tasks bar, select the file, and then click Rename This File in the File And Folder Tasks bar. Windows places a box around the document name and highlights the current name. Type the new document name you want, and then click outside the box.

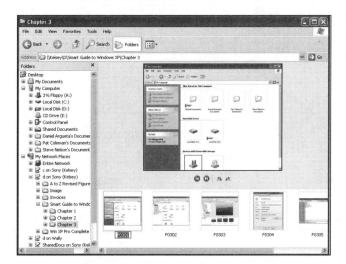

FIGURE 3-7

The My Computer folder showing a renaming text box.

Note You can't rename Windows system files and folder. Don't rename program files; only rename document files. If you rename program files, your programs may not start correctly.

Renaming Folders

You rename a folder in the same way that you rename a file. Open the My Computer folder, and find the folder. Once you find the folder, use any of the methods described in the previous section to rename it.

Creating New Folders

You can create new folders to better organize your documents. For example, if you know you'll be creating many documents and you want to segregate your documents into three categories—letters, reports, and memos—you would create three separate folders. To create a new folder, follow these steps:

1 Display the list of disks or folders into which you want to place the new folder. For example, if you want to create a new folder for your C disk, display the contents—this will be its files and folders—of the C disk using the My Computer folder. And if you want to create a new subfolder inside the My Documents folder, display the contents of the My Documents folder using the My Computer window.

2 Select the folder into which you want to create the new folder.

3 Choose the File menu's New command to display the New submenu, and then choose the Folder command (see Figure 3-8). Windows creates a new folder or subfolder.

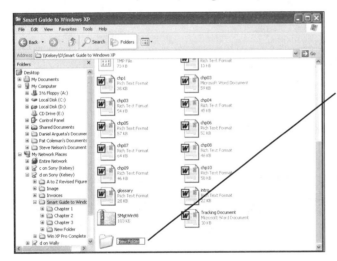

FIGURE 3-8

The My Computer folder with the File menu's New submenu showing and a newly created folder entitled "New Folder."

The new folder.

4 Name the folder.

Note After you create a new folder, you'll want to move or copy documents to it. The later chapter sections "Moving Documents" and "Copying Documents" describe how you do this.

Deleting Documents

To delete a file, select it, and then do one of the following:

• Press the Delete key.

- Click the Delete button on the toolbar.
- Click the Delete This File link in the File And Folder Tasks bar.

You can also delete a file by right-clicking it and choosing Delete from the shortcut menu.

Note Never delete program files. If you want to remove a program, use the Control Panel's Add/Remove programs tool, which is described in Chapter 10, "Customizing Windows XP."

When you delete a file, Windows doesn't actually remove it from your disk. Instead, Windows moves the file to a special folder named the Recycle Bin. Periodically—and usually only when the Recycle Bin gets full—Windows removes a file from this folder.

Note For more information about the Recycle Bin, refer to the later chapter section "Emptying Your Recycle Bin."

Deleting a Folder

You can delete a folder, which means you delete all the files in the folder and the folder too. To delete a folder, use any of the methods described in the previous section for deleting a file.

Undoing a File or Folder Command

Most of the time, you can reverse the effect of your last, or most recent, file or folder command. For example, if you've just renamed a file or folder, you can undo the renaming. If you've just moved or copied a file, you can put everything back into its original place or condition. If you've just deleted a file or folder, you can undo this operation. To undo your last file or folder command, click the Edit menu, and choose Undo *Action* (the word "Action" stands for your most recent action—Rename, Move, Copy, or Delete).

Undeleting Documents

You can also undelete, or restore, a file or folder you've previously deleted by using the Recycle Bin. To do this, double-click the Recycle Bin shortcut icon, which appears on the Windows desktop. When Windows displays the contents of the Recycle Bin folder, as shown in Figure 3-9 (next page), use one of the following methods to restore the file:

- Find the document you want to undelete, right-click it, and then choose the shortcut menu's Restore command.
- Select the file, and then click Restore This Item in the Recycle Bin Tasks bar.

Regardless of the method you use, the file is restored to its original location, that is, if it had been in a subfolder of your My Documents folder, you will now find it there again.

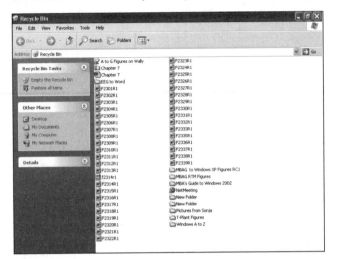

FIGURE 3-9

The Recycle Bin folder temporarily stores the files you've deleted.

If you want to restore several document files at once, first select all the files. You can select multiple files by holding down the Ctrl key and then clicking each file you want to select. In List view, you can also draw a box around the documents you want to restore by clicking the mouse in a space beyond one of the documents and holding down the left button. As you move the mouse, Windows will draw a dotted box. Move the mouse to stretch this box to enclose all the files you want to restore, and then release the button. Now use one of the methods described earlier in this section to restore the files.

Moving Documents

Using the My Computer folder, you can move a document from one disk to another disk and from one folder to another folder in any of the following ways:

- Right-click the document name, and then choose Cut from the shortcut menu. Now right-click the folder into which you want to place the document, and choose Paste from the shortcut menu.
- Select the document name, and then click Move This File in the File And Folder Tasks bar to open the Move Items dialog box (see Figure 3-10). Select the folder into which you want to place the document, and click the Move button.

FIGURE 3-10

The Move Items dialog box.

- Select the document name, click the Edit menu, and then choose Cut. Select the folder into which you want to place the document, click the Edit menu, and then choose Paste.
- Select the document name, and press Ctrl+X. Select the folder into which you want to place the document, and press Ctrl+V.
- Click the document name to select it, and then drag it to the folder into which you want to place the document.
- Right-click the document name to select it, and then drag it to the folder into which you want to place the document. Release the mouse button to display a shortcut menu, and then choose Move Here.

Note that you can easily move several document files at once. To do so, select all the files before clicking the Cut button. You can select multiple files by holding down the Ctrl key and then clicking each file you want to select. You can also draw a box around the documents you want to move by dragging the mouse between the opposite corners of an imaginary box that contains all of the documents you want to move. To select all the files in the folder, choose the Edit menu's Select All command or press Ctrl+A. Now move the documents using any of the methods described in this section.

Copying Documents

You can also copy a document from one disk to another disk and from one folder to another folder. When you copy a document, the original document stays in its original location. You move a duplicate copy to another disk or folder. You can copy a document in the following ways:

- Right-click the document name, and then choose Copy from the shortcut menu. Now right-click the folder into which you want to place the document, and choose Paste from the shortcut menu.
- Select the document name, and then click Copy This File in the File And Folder Tasks bar to open the Copy Items dialog box (see Figure 3-11). Select the folder into which you want to place the document, and click the Copy button.

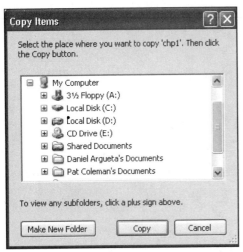

FIGURE 3-11

The Copy Items dialog box.

- Select the document name, click the Edit menu, and then choose Copy. Select the folder into which you want to place the document, click the Edit menu, and then choose Paste.
- Select the document name, and press Ctrl+C. Select the folder into which you want to place the document, and press Ctrl+V.
- Right-click the document name, and then drag it to the folder into which you want to place the document. Release the mouse button to display a shortcut menu, and choose Copy Here.

To copy several document files at once, select all the files before clicking the Copy button. As noted earlier, you can select multiple files by holding down the Ctrl key and then clicking each file you want to select. In List view, you can also draw a box around the documents you want to copy by dragging the mouse between the opposite corners of an imaginary box that contains all of the documents you want to copy. To select all the files in the folder, choose the Edit menu's Select All command or press Ctrl+A.

Opening Documents on a Network

The earlier discussions in this chapter implicitly assume you're working with Windows on a stand-alone desktop or laptop computer. But I want to point out that everything I've said about opening documents, moving documents, copying documents, and so forth also applies to working on a network. A network is just a group of computers that have been connected in a way that lets the people who use the computers share files, folders, and disks.

To view the files, folders, and disks available to you through a network, use the My Network Places window (see Figure 3-12). To open this window, click Start and then click My Network Places.

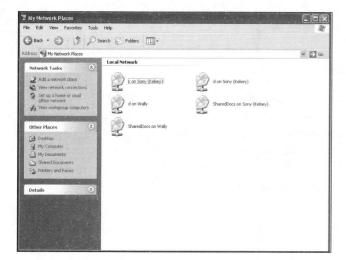

FIGURE 3-12

The My Network Places window lets you view the drives on the other computers connected to the network.

Each computer on a network gets a name, as shown in Figure 3-12. On the little network in my office, for example, I have computers named Wally and Kelsey.

To see the folders and files that a network disk stores, double-click its folders. Figure 3-13 (next page) shows the folders and files on C on Kelsey. Note that once you get to this My Network Places window, you work with files and folders in the same manner as you work with files and folders on a local disk. A local disk is just a computer disk that's inside the computer you're working on.

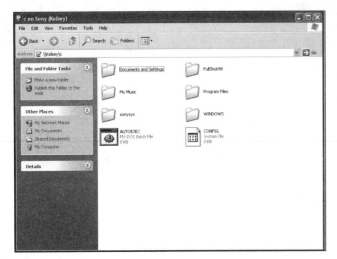

FIGURE 3-13

This My Network Places window shows the files and folders available on Kelsey's C disk.

Note

You don't automatically get to do whatever you want with network disks. First of all, other people need to say it's okay to share their local disks in order to make them available to the network. And then, even after saying sharing is okay, what you can do over the network is usually limited. For example, you may be able to view a document or copy it, but you probably won't be able to delete it or rename it. If you have additional questions about how information sharing works on your network, consult the network administrator.

Performing Housekeeping Tasks

Before we wrap up this discussion of files, folders, and disks, we should talk about a handful of related housekeeping tasks. Specifically, you want to know how to empty the Recycle Bin, how to format floppy disks, how to back up your files so that you reduce the risk of losing important information, how to burn CDs, and how to compress files.

Emptying Your Recycle Bin

If your disk space is limited, you'll want to empty your Recycle Bin when it becomes full of files you know that you'll never need again. By doing this, you free up wasted space. In some cases, you even modestly improve the performance of Windows.

To empty your Recycle Bin, follow these steps:

1 Double-click the Recycle Bin shortcut icon on the Windows desktop. Windows displays the contents of the Recycle Bin folder (see Figure 3-14).

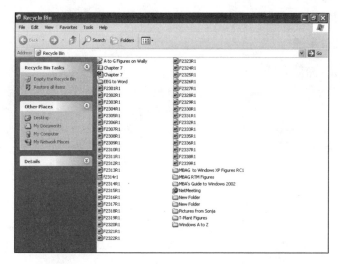

FIGURE 3-14

The Recycle Bin folder.

2 Verify that the Recycle Bin folder doesn't hold files that you may later want to restore. If it does, restore them as described earlier in this chapter.

3 In the Recycle Bin Tasks bar, click the Empty The Recycle Bin link.

Note You can tell how full your hard disk is—and therefore whether you need to free up space by emptying your Recycle Bin—by opening the My Computer folder and then clicking the disk. When you do this, Windows displays information about the disk in the Details bar, including the file system used on the disk, the amount of free space, and the total size of the disk.

Formatting a Floppy Disk

You won't need to format your hard disk—the computer manufacturer does that for you. If you purchase formatted floppy disks, you don't need to format them either before you can use them. But you may need to format floppy disks for a couple of reasons: (1) you purchased unformatted disks; (2) you want to erase the data on the disk and use the disk again.

To format a floppy disk, place the disk in its drive, and then follow these steps:

1 Open the My Computer folder.

2 Right-click the floppy disk icon.

3 Choose the shortcut menu's Format command. Windows displays the Format dialog box (see Figure 3-15 on the next page).

FIGURE 3-15

The Format dialog box.

4 Confirm that the Capacity drop-down list box shows the correct floppy disk capacity. If it doesn't, click the down arrow to activate the list box and select the correct capacity from the list. If you're unsure of the floppy disk's capacity, you may need to experiment by trying both capacity choices.

5 In the Format Options section, select the type of formatting you want:

- Quick Format—Select this option if you've formatted the disk before and now want to only delete its files.

- Enable Compression—Select this option if you want to compress the files and folders on the disk. This option is available only on NTFS formatted drives. It is not available for floppy drives.

- Create An MS-DOS Startup Disk—Select this option to make the disk a bootable disk—a disk you can use to start your computer and the MS-DOS operating system.

Note You typically don't need to fill in or select the other boxes.

---

6 Click the Start button. Windows formats the floppy disk according to your specifications. Click the Close button, and then click the Cancel button to return to the My Computer folder.

Backing Up Files

Although your computer's disks are generally reliable, you don't want take chances with your information. For this reason, you'll want to keep backup, or duplicate, copies of your important document files. You can do this in a variety of ways, but the simplest way is to copy your important document files to another disk such as a floppy disk. For example, to back up the contents of the My Documents folder, you can copy its files, or even the entire folder, to a floppy disk or a set of floppy disks. (If you have numerous documents stored in the My Documents folder, you may need several floppy disks to hold all your information.)

Note You typically don't need to keep backup copies of your program files because these are relatively easy to replace. For example, if a program file gets fouled up, you can just reinstall the program using the original CD or set of floppy disks. (Chapter 10, "Customizing Windows XP," talks in detail about how you do this.) And if the original CD or floppy disks become unusable, you can usually get a replacement copy from the software manufacturer for a nominal sum if you have registered your software.

If you have huge numbers of documents to back up, by the way, you can also acquire more sophisticated backup devices such as tape storage units and removable hard disks. These high-capacity storage units can store 100 to 3,000 times as much information as a single floppy disk. Or, if you have a recordable CD drive, you can back up to a CD, as described in the next section.

Burning CDs

If you bought your computer recently, it probably came with a recordable CD drive, and if you have lots of data files on your system, copying these files to a CD (called "burning") is the most effective and efficient method for ensuring that you have a reliable backup. To copy data files to a CD, follow these steps:

1 Open the My Computer folder and select the files or folders you want to copy.

2 Place a blank recordable CD in the CD drive. In most cases (depending on how your system is set up), you'll see the dialog box shown in Figure 3-16 (next page). Click Open Writable CD Folder Using Windows Explorer. To skip this step in the future, also click the Always Do The Selected Action check box, and then click OK.

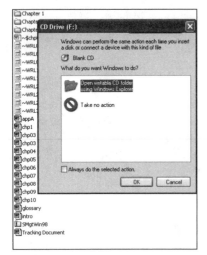

FIGURE 3-16

Starting the process to burn a CD.

3 Now you need to copy the files you want to burn to the CD, and you can do so in a few ways:

- Right-click the file you want to copy (or select a folder or multiple files), and from the shortcut menu choose Send To and then click CD-Drive.
- Drag the files and drop them on the CD drive in the My Computer folder.

Whichever method you use, you'll then see the window shown in Figure 3-17.

FIGURE 3-17

The CD Drive window.

4 In the CD Writing Tasks bar, click Write These Files To CD to start the CD Writing Wizard, which is shown in Figure 3-18.

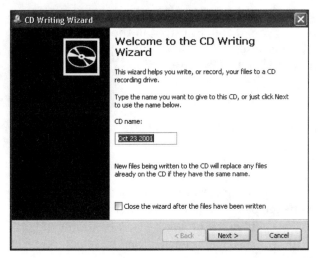

FIGURE 3-18

The CD Writing Wizard.

5 Enter a name for the CD in the CD Name box, and then click Next. The Wizard then starts copying the file or files. A progress indicator tells you how much time is left.

6 When the file copy is complete, click Finish.

7 Check in your My Computer folder that all the files you intended to copy have been copied and that they are accessible.

To copy a file back to your hard drive, use the methods you learned earlier in this chapter for copying any file or folder.

Note If you change your mind about copying something to a CD, click the Delete Temporary Files link in the Tasks bar. Windows displays the Confirm Delete dialog box. Click Yes. You are not deleting the file from your hard drive but only from its temporary holding area.

Compressing Files and Folders

Compressing a file or folder decreases its size so that it takes up less space on a drive or transfers quicker. A number of compression programs are available through third-party vendors as shareware or commercial products. Included with Windows XP, however, is WinZip7, a popular compression utility that has been widely distributed in previous versions.

To compress a file, right-click it in your My Computer folder, click Send To on the shortcut menu, and then click Compressed Folder. A compressed copy is placed in the folder that contains the original file. You can easily identify it because its file folder icon displays a closed zipper (see Figure 3-19). To unzip the file, double-click it. You can also compress a file by dragging it to a compressed folder.

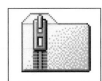

FIGURE 3-19

A zipper identifies compressed folders.

To compress a folder, right-click it, click Send To on the shortcut menu, and then click Compressed Folder. A zipped folder is placed in the parent folder of the original folder. If you want a compressed folder in a location other than where the program places it, simply drag it there or used the Cut and Paste commands. You can also compress files and folders in Windows applications, such as Outlook Express, as you'll see in Chapter 5.

Chapter 4

Printing

You will want to print many of the documents you create with Microsoft Windows XP and Windows programs, so this chapter talks about printing with Windows. Specifically, this chapter describes the following tasks:

- Adding printers
- Printing
- Working with the Printers And Faxes folder
- Changing fonts

Adding Printers

To use a printer, you need to do more than just connect your computer to the printer with a cable. You need to provide Windows with enough information about the printer so that Windows knows how to use the printer.

To provide Windows with this information, you add the printer to the Printers And Faxes folder. The Printers And Faxes folder isn't like a regular folder. As you may already know or remember from Chapter 3, folders typically store files. The Printers And Faxes folder, however, stores descriptions of the printers that you've said you want to use.

Note   For more information on what folders are and how Windows uses them to store **files,** refer to Chapter 3.

One other quick comment: If a printer connects directly to your computer, Windows calls the printer a local printer. To add the local printer to your Printers And Faxes folder, follow the first set of instructions provided below. If your computer connects to a network and the network includes printers, you can also use these printers—they're called network printers—to print. To add a network printer to your Printers And Faxes folder, follow the second set of instructions provided below.

Adding a Local Plug-and-Play Printer

To add a local printer that is Plug and Play, first verify the printer cable is securely connected to both the printer and your computer. Make sure you've followed whatever setup instructions the printer manufacturer has supplied, and then follow these steps:

1 Turn the printer on.

2 Click the Start button, and then click Printers And Faxes to open the Printers And Faxes folder (see Figure 4-1).

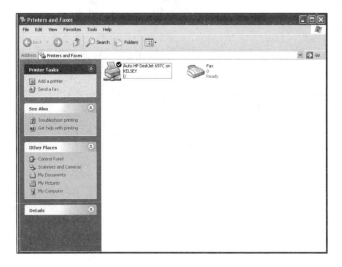

FIGURE 4-1

The Printers And Faxes folder.

3 In the Printer Tasks bar, click the Add A Printer link to start the Add Printer Wizard.

4 When Windows displays the Welcome screen (not shown here), click the Next button. Windows displays the Local Or Network Printer screen (see Figure 4-2).

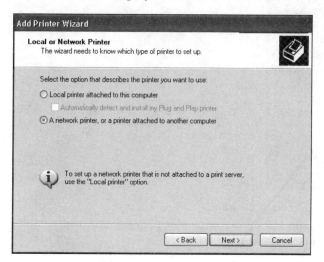

FIGURE 4-2

The Wizard asks whether you want to add a local printer or a network printer.

4

Note Click the Back button if you want to move to the previous Add Printer Wizard dialog box.

---

5 Click the Local Printer Attached To This Computer option button, click the Automatically Detect And Install My Plug And Play Printer check box, and then click the Next button. The Wizard will then automatically detect and install your printer. Back in the Printers And Faxes folder you'll see an icon for the printer.

Adding a Local Printer That Is Not Plug and Play

If you have an older printer that is not Plug and Play, follow these steps to install it:

1 Turn the printer on.

2 Click the Start button, and then click Printers And Faxes to open the Printers And Faxes folder.

3 In the Printer Tasks bar, click the Add A Printer link to start the Add Printer Wizard.

4 When Windows displays the Welcome screen, click the Next button to display the Local Or Network Printer screen.

5 Click the Local Printer Attached To This Computer option button, and then click Next to display the Select A Printer Port screen (see Figure 4-3 on the next page).

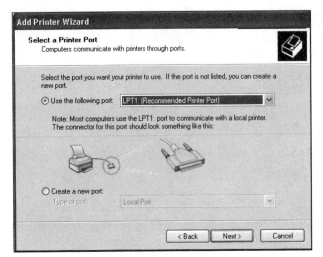

FIGURE 4-3

Selecting a printer port.

6 Click the Use The Following Port option button, and leave LPT1 selected in the drop-down list box unless you know that your computer communicates with a printer using a different port. Click Next to display the Install Printer Software screen (see Figure 4-4).

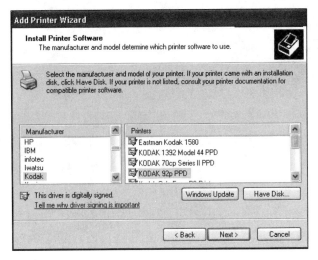

FIGURE 4-4

Identifying your printer.

7 Select the name of the company that manufactured your printer from the Manufacturers list box.

8 Select the name of the printer model from the Printers list box, and then click Next to open the Name Your Printer screen (see Figure 4-5).

Note If you don't see your printer's manufacturer or the printer model listed, you need to do slightly more work to add the printer. If your printer came with a floppy disk labeled something like "Windows printer drivers" or "Printer installation disk," insert that floppy disk into the floppy disk drive, click the Have Disk button, and press the Enter key. If your printer didn't come with a setup floppy disk, use the printer's user manual to find out which common printer your printer emulates, or mimics. Once you learn what other printer your printer emulates, select that printer manufacturer and printer model from the list boxes shown in Figure 4-4. Note that you may need to do something—like flip a switch or follow some simple set of instructions—in order to tell your printer it should emulate this other, popular printer.

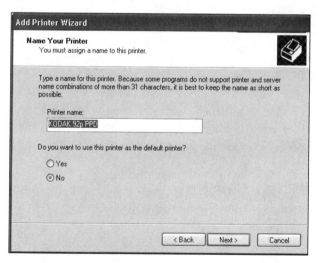

FIGURE 4-5

Assigning a name to your printer.

9 Use the Printer Name text box to give the printer a name you'll recognize. Or, alternatively, use whatever Windows suggests.

10 If this printer will be your principal printer—in other words, the one that you want to use most often—click the Yes option button to answer the question "Do you want to use this printer as the default printer?" and then click the Next button to display the Printer Sharing screen (see Figure 4-6).

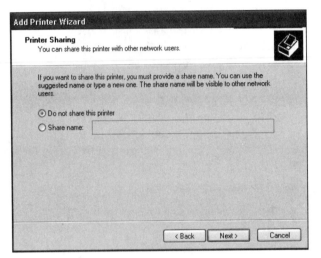

FIGURE 4-6

If your computer is on a network, you can share it with other users.

11 If your computer is part of a network and you want to share it with other users, click the Share Name option button and then give the printer a name that will identify it. If your computer is not part of a network or you don't want to share the printer, click the Do Not Share This Printer option button. Click Next to display the Print Test Page screen (see Figure 4-7).

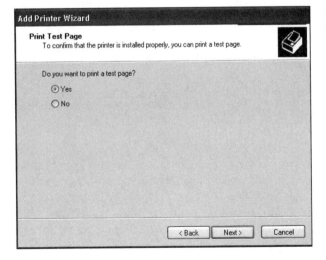

FIGURE 4-7

Printing a test page is a good idea.

12 Click the Yes option button to answer the question "Do you want to print a test page?" and click the Next button.

13 Verify that Windows correctly prints the test page, and then click Finish. Almost always, Windows prints the test page correctly. If Windows doesn't print the test page correctly, don't worry. When Windows completes printing the test page, it will ask whether the page printed correctly. If you answer the question "No," Windows displays a laundry list of fix-it steps you can take. In those rare cases when you can't get the test page to print correctly, you can almost always get the printer to work by following Windows' fix-it suggestions.

Note If you still can't get a printer to work even after you've carefully followed the instructions provided here and after you've implemented whatever suggestions Windows has made, find the user's manual that came with the printer, locate the printer manufacturer's technical support telephone number, and then call them.

Adding a Network Printer

As mentioned earlier in the chapter, you can print documents using both local printers connected to your computer and network printers, which are just printers connected to other computers on the network. However, in order to use a network printer, you do need to add it to your Printers And Faxes folder.

To add a network printer, follow these steps:

1 Verify that the network printer is turned on. What's more, verify that it's okay for you to use the network printer. (To do this, you'll need to ask the network administrator.)

2 Click the Start button, and then click Printers And Faxes to open the Printers And Faxes folder.

3 In the Printer Tasks bar, click Add A Printer to start the Add Printer Wizard.

4 At the Welcome screen, click Next to display the Local Or Network Printer screen.

5 Click the A Network Printer, Or A Printer Attached To Another Computer option button, and then click the Next button to display the Specify A Printer screen (see Figure 4-8 on next page).

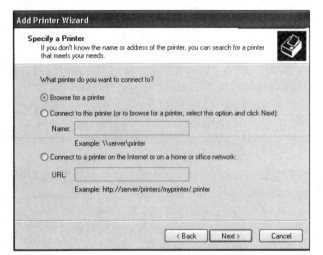

FIGURE 4-8

Specifying a network printer.

6 You can specify the network printer you want to connect to in three ways:

- In most cases, leave the Browse For A Printer option button selected, click Next, and follow the procedure described in the next steps here.
- If you know the printer's name and location on the network, you can click the Connect To This Printer option and supply the path, which will be something like \\Wally\HP DeskJet.
- If the printer has a URL and you know it, you can select the Connect To A Printer On The Internet Or On A Home Or Office Network option button and then supply the URL.
- If you select Browse For A Printer and click Next, the Wizard displays the Browse For Printer screen (see Figure 4-9).

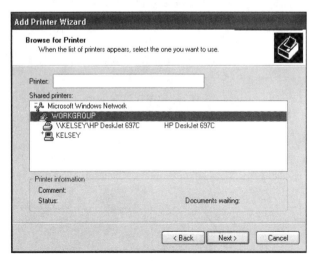

FIGURE 4-9

The Browse For Printer screen.

7 Click the network printer you want to add. If you don't see any network printers, you may need to expand the network diagram shown in Figure 4-9 so that it shows not only computers but also networked printers. To do this, click the plus signs (+) next to the computer names. When you've selected the network printer from the Browse For Printer dialog box, click Next to display the Default Printer screen (see Figure 4-10).

Note If you don't see the network printer listed in the Browse For Printer dialog box, you probably have one of two problems. First, the problem may be that your network administrator hasn't told Windows it's okay for the printer to be shared. If this is the problem, ask the network administrator to share the printer. If Windows already knows a printer is okay to use as a network printer—say, the network administrator has already shared the printer—the problem may be that Windows can't see the computer or the printer. If this is the problem, ask the network administrator for the pathname that points to the computer and printer.

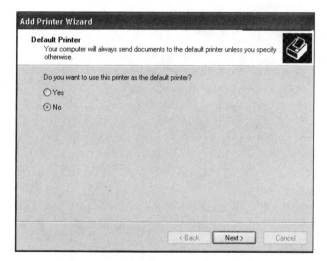

FIGURE 4-10

Click Yes if you want to always use the network printer.

8 If this printer will be your principal printer—in other words, the one that you want to use most often—click the Yes option button to answer the question "Do you want to use this printer as the default printer?" and then click the Next button to open the summary screen. If the information is correct, click Finish. Otherwise, you can click the Back button to find a screen and make changes.

Printing

Once you've added a local or network printer, you can use it to print documents. You can print documents right from Windows, which is handy when you want to print a document that already exists. Or you can print documents from inside programs, which is more often the case, because you'll frequently want to print a document while you're working with it. I'll describe how both techniques work in the following paragraphs.

Printing from Windows

To print a document from Windows without starting the program you used to create the document, first use the My Computer or the My Network Places folder to find the disk or folder and the document. When you've found the document you want to print, right-click it and choose the shortcut menu's Print command (see Figure 4-11). When you choose the Print command, Windows starts the program you originally used to create the document, tells it to open and print the document, and then stops the program.

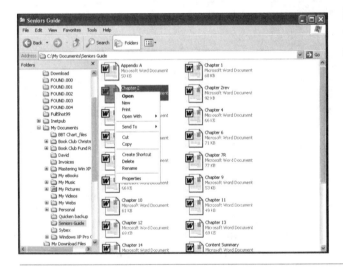

FIGURE 4-11

The My Computer folder with the shortcut menu displayed.

Note If you have questions about how the My Computer or My Network Places folders work, refer to Chapter 3, "Files, Folders, and Disks."

Printing from Within a Program

To print a document from within a program, you first need to start and open the document. Then you need to issue the print command to the program. How you issue this command depends on the program. In general, however, a program's File menu provides a Print command, so choose the File menu's Print command. When the program displays its Print dialog box (see Figure 4-12), you use it to describe how you want to print the document. Figure 4-12, for example, shows the Print dialog box that the WordPad accessory program displays.

FIGURE 4-12

The Print dialog box.

4

Note   If you have questions about how to start a program or open a document, refer to Chapter 1, "Starting Windows XP," and Chapter 3, "Files, Folders, and Disks."

Because the WordPad Print dialog box resembles the dialog boxes provided by other programs, let me make a few quick comments. Typically, a Print dialog box provides a Select Printer box that contains icons and the names of the printers installed on your system. Select an icon to specify which printer Windows should use to print the document. Windows initially suggests a printer—this is the default printer we talked about briefly earlier in the discussion of adding printers—but you can select any other printer you've added.

The Print dialog box also typically provides other boxes and buttons you use to specify how a document should be printed. For example, most Print dialog boxes include a Number Of Copies box that you can use to indicate how many copies you want to print. Programs that let you create lengthy documents also provide buttons and boxes you can use to specify which pages you want to print.

Printing Photos

Windows XP includes a Photo Printing Wizard that you can use to print photographs from a digital camera or a scanner or other photographs or images stored on your computer. To start the Wizard, click the Start button, click My Pictures, select a folder of pictures, and then click Print Pictures from the Picture Tasks bar. At the Welcome screen, click Next, and then follow these steps:

1 In the Picture Selection screen, which is shown in Figure 4-13, clear the checkmarks from the pictures you don't want to print, and then click Next.

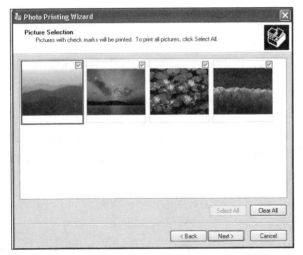

FIGURE 4-13

The Picture Selection screen.

2 In the Printing Options screen, tell the Wizard which printer to use and the type of paper, and then click Next.

3 In the Layout Selection screen, tell the Wizard how to size and format your photo(s). The Print Preview box will show you how your selection will look when printed. Click Next.

The Wizard then sends your photo(s) to the printer, and they are printed.

Working with the Printers And Faxes Folder

I talked a bit about the Printers And Faxes folder at the beginning of this chapter. As mentioned earlier, you use the Add A Printer link in the Printer Tasks bar of the Printers And Faxes folder to start the wizard and describe the local and network printers you want Windows to use. The Printers And Faxes folder, however, actually does more than this. The Printers And Faxes folder also stores descriptions of these printers, the settings you want Windows to use with a printer, and a list of the documents you've sent to a printer.

Most of these details aren't all that relevant to typical users—people like you and me. But there are a few things you'll want to know: how to view and manage the documents lined up in a printer's queue and how to customize a printer's properties.

Managing a Printer Queue

When you tell Windows or another program that you want to print a document, what actually happens is that Windows creates a printable copy of the document—it's called a spool file—and then carefully passes the pages of this spool file to your printer so that it can print them. If you print a short, simple document, this process happens very quickly. So quickly, in fact, that you can't really watch it happen. If you print a long document or one that Windows or the printer takes a long time to handle—this happens with documents that use lots of fancy graphics or color—you can actually watch the process and even monitor the printing process's progress.

To see what document a printer is printing and how far along it is in the printing, follow these steps:

1 Click the Start button, and then click Printers And Faxes to open the Printers And Faxes folder.

2 Double-click the icon for the printer you want to monitor. Windows opens a window that shows the documents sitting in the printer's queue (see Figure 4-14 on the next page).

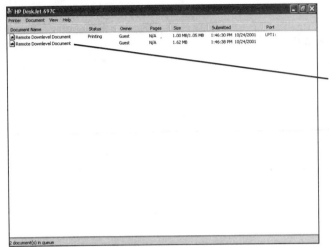

FIGURE 4-14

This window shows the documents that Windows has sent to the printer to be printed.

This document is waiting to print.

You'll want to know how to perform several handy tasks using the window shown in Figure 4-14. So I'll quickly tell you how to take care of some tasks.

Windows arranges printing documents in the order in which they were sent to the printer queue, but you can actually rearrange them in a different order. To do so, click the column heading buttons—Document Name, Status, Owner, Pages, Size, Submitted, and Port—that appear beneath the title bar. If you click the Document Name button, for example, Windows arranges the printing documents in alphabetical order. If you click the Document Name button again, Windows arranges the printing documents in reverse alphabetical order. The other column heading buttons work in a similar fashion, so if you have questions, just experiment with them.

You can cancel and pause the printing of a document. To tell Windows not to print a document, right-click the document and then choose the shortcut menu's Cancel command. To tell Windows to wait to print a document, right-click the document and then choose the shortcut menu's Pause command. To tell Windows to restart printing a document you previously told it to wait to print, right-click the document and then choose the Restart command.

You can pause and restart a printer, which means you effectively stop the printing of all documents. To tell Windows to stop the printer from printing all documents, choose the Printer menu's Pause Printing command. To tell Windows to restart a printer you previously told it to pause, choose the Printer menu's Pause Printing command again.

Note   The Printer menu's Pause Printing command works like a toggle switch. When the switch is on, because you've paused the printer, Windows marks the command with a check.

As you may remember from this chapter's earlier discussion of adding local and network printers, one printer in your Printers And Faxes folder is the default printer. Windows suggests this default printer when it displays a Print dialog box after you choose the File menu's Print command. Windows also automatically uses the default printer when you don't specify a printer—say, because you're printing from Windows or you issued the print command by clicking the Print toolbar button. To tell Windows to make the selected printer the default printer, right-click the printer's icon and choose the shortcut menu's Set As Default command. Or choose the Printer menu's Set As Default Printer command.

Sometimes you'll want to issue a print command even though a printer isn't actually available or connected to your computer. If you're at home working on a laptop, for example, you might want to issue print commands for the documents you're working on—even though the laptop isn't yet connected to a printer. Perhaps you'll reconnect the laptop to a printer when you get back to your office. You can actually do this sort of time-delayed printing by using Windows' offline printing feature. In essence, with offline printing, Windows waits to send a print document to a printer's queue until you've said you're back online.

To tell Windows that you want to wait to send documents to a printer's queue before you issue the print command, choose the Printer menu's Use Printer Offline command. To tell Windows to go back online and move any print documents you created when you were offline to the Printers And Faxes folder, choose the Printer menu's Use Printer Offline command again.

Note The Use Printer Offline command also works like a toggle switch. When the switch is on, because you've indicated you want to use offline printing, Windows marks the command with a check.

There's one final trick you'll want to know how to do. You can simultaneously delete all the documents that are printing or waiting to print in the document queue. To tell Windows to remove all of the printing and paused documents from the print queue, choose the Printer menu's Cancel All Documents command.

Note If you issue the Cancel All Documents command to a network printer, you can delete other people's print documents if you have enough authority. Therefore, you'll want to be careful about issuing this command.

Customizing a Printer's Properties

Customizing a printer's properties quickly becomes a very esoteric subject because each printer is different. What's more, the way your printer works right out of the box is typically the way you want it to work. Nevertheless, you'll benefit from having some general knowledge of this subject.

To make changes to the way a printer works, follow these steps:

1 Click the Start button, and then click Printers And Faxes to open the Printers And Faxes folder.

2 Right-click the icon for the printer you want to customize, and choose Properties from the shortcut menu to open the Properties dialog box for that printer (see Figure 4-15).

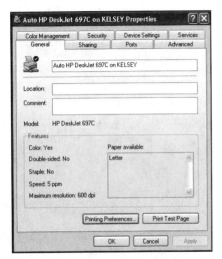

FIGURE 4-15

A printer's Properties dialog box displaying the General tab.

Then use the printer's Properties dialog box to customize the way the printer works. One important point to note is that because different printers give you different customization options, the Properties dialog boxes for different printers look different. If you display the Properties dialog box for your printer, for example, it'll probably look different from the one shown in Figure 4-15 (unless you happen to have the same printer).

Even though different printers provide different Properties dialog boxes, several similarities exist in the way in which these dialog boxes work. For example, first of all, note that you can print a test page to verify that a printer works correctly by clicking the General tab and then clicking the Print Test Page button. If you question whether your printer is working correctly, therefore, you can use this tactic to confirm your printer's operability—or its inoperability.

Another handy customization concerns changing the printer's paper specifications. In the printer's Properties dialog box on the General tab, click the Preference button to open the Preferences dialog box for that printer, and then click the Paper/Quality tab. This tab—assuming your printer supplies this tab—allows you to specify the type of paper you want to use in your printer. As Figure 4-16 shows, the Paper/Quality tab provides several clickable buttons and icons you can use to specify which type of paper the printer uses and how the printer should print on the paper.

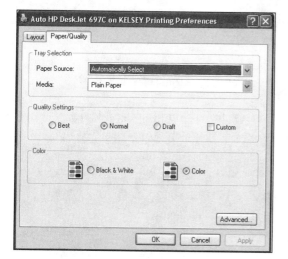

FIGURE 4-16

The Paper/Quality tab typically looks something like this.

A Word about Fonts

When you print, you use a particular typeface, or font. Examples of fonts included with Windows XP include Comic Sans MS (a popular font for use in Web pages), Courier (which looks like a typewriter did the printing), and Times New Roman (the default font for printing in Windows applications). To see the entire selection of fonts, follow these steps:

1 Click the Start button, and then click Control Panel to open Control Panel (see Figure 4-17 on the next page).

FIGURE 4-17

Control Panel in Category view.

Note You can open Control Panel in two views: Category and Classic. Chapter 10 explains Control Panel and shows how to use the programs in it to customize Windows XP.

2 In the Explorer bar, click the Switch To Classic View link to open Control Panel in Classic view, the view that will look familiar to you if you've used previous versions of Windows

3 Double-click Fonts to open the Fonts folder (see Figure 4-18).

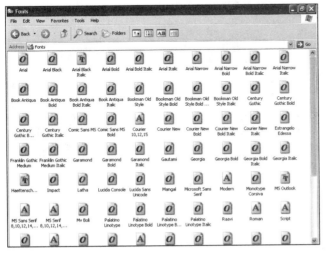

FIGURE 4-18

The Fonts folder.

You'll notice that fonts are identified with a lettered icon, which indicates the type of font. Windows XP provides three types of fonts:

- The icon containing the letter O indicates an Open Type font, which looks the same on the screen and when printed. An Open Type font can be rotated and scaled to various sizes.

- The icon containing the letters TT indicates a TrueType font. This font also looks the same on the screen and when printed.

- The icon containing the letter A indicates either a vector font or a raster font. Vector fonts are used primarily with plotters, and raster fonts are stored as bitmap images. They cannot be scaled or rotated and won't print if your printer doesn't support them.

A font can have size, which is measured in points (1 point is 1/72 inch), and style (for example, italic or boldface). To see what a particular font looks like in various sizes, double-click its icon.

To display a list of fonts that are similar, select a font, click the View menu, and then click List Fonts By Similarity. To display only the basic fonts and not all variations, such as roman, italic, bold, bold italic, and so on, click the View menu, and then click Hide Variations.

Changing the Font in an Application

To change the default font and print a document in a font that you specify, you must print from an application. The steps are the same in most Windows applications. Follow these steps to specify the font for a printed document in WordPad:

1 Click the Start button, click All Programs, click Accessories, and then click WordPad to open WordPad.

2 Click the Format menu, and then click Font to open the Font dialog box, which is shown in Figure 4-19.

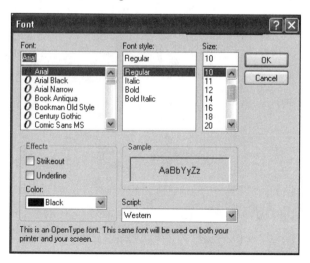

FIGURE 4-19

The Font dialog box.

3 Select a font, a font style, a size, a color, and an effect, and then click OK.

Installing a New Font

Although Windows XP comes with a great many fonts in all sorts of styles and sizes, you may want to install other fonts for special purposes. To install a new font, follow these steps:

1 In the Fonts folder, click the File menu, and then click Install New Font to open the Add Fonts dialog box, as shown in Figure 4-20.

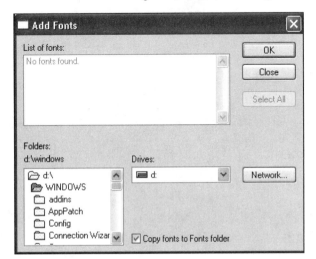

FIGURE 4-20

The Add Fonts dialog box.

2 In the Drives drop-down list box, select the drive where the font is stored, and click OK. By default, fonts are copied to the Fonts folder.

Chapter 5

Communicating on the Internet

Microsoft Windows XP provides numerous tools for working with the Internet. Now, in truth, one could write an entire book about using Windows XP's Internet features. In this book, however, I'm going to devote only two chapters to the Internet. This chapter starts a discussion of Windows and the Internet by talking about the following subjects:

- Explaining the Internet (in big-picture terms)
- Connecting to the Internet
- Sending and receiving e-mail
- Working with newsgroups
- Instant Messaging with Windows Messenger

Note In the next chapter, I describe how you can use the Internet to share information and files using the **World Wide Web.**

What Is the Internet? – The Big Picture

Let's start this chapter by describing what the Internet is as well as what it allows you to do. Think of the Internet as a big, loosely organized network that connects computers and networks from around the world. People get excited about this—sometimes perhaps more than they should—because the Internet allows people to communicate and share information and resources. By information, I mean files, and by resources, I mean disk storage space and sometimes computer time. But in a nutshell, that's really it. And once you're connected to the Internet, you can begin sharing information and resources with other Internet users, too.

Connecting to the Internet

Before you can begin using the Internet, you need to connect your computer to the Internet. These days you can connect to your computer in several ways. The most common, yet the slowest, is through a telephone line and a dial-up modem. More and more people, though, have access to a broadband connection, either via cable or DSL (Digital Subscriber Line), and broadband connections can be, in theory, as much as 1000 times faster than the fastest dial-up modem. Another type of connection that is faster than a dial-up connection but not as fast as a broadband connection is ISDN (Integrated Services Digital Network). In this section, I'll explain all of these kinds of connections and show you how to set them up in Windows XP.

Note A broadband connection is simply a connection that uses a high-speed device.

Note If you work on a computer that provides a permanent connection to the Internet, such as through a local area network, you don't need to make a connection in order to use the Internet. You're already connected to the Internet. If you have questions about how this permanent connection works, ask your network administrator.

Connecting with a Telephone Modem

If the modem in your computer is Plug and Play, you don't need to install it. Windows XP recognized it and installed it automatically during the installation of the operating system. You do need to create an Internet connection for the modem, however, and you'll need an account with an ISP (Internet Service Provider). Once you have this account, you'll need some information in order to set up your connection: the telephone number the modem must dial and your user name and password. To set up your connection, follow these steps:

1 Click the Start button, click All Programs, click Accessories, click Communications, and then click New Connection Wizard to start the New Connection Wizard.

2 At the Welcome screen, click Next to display the Network Connection Type screen, shown in Figure 5-1.

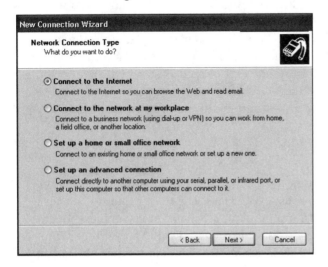

FIGURE 5-1

Telling the Wizard that you want to connect to the Internet.

3 Click the Connect To The Internet option button, and then click Next to display the Getting Ready screen, shown in Figure 5-2.

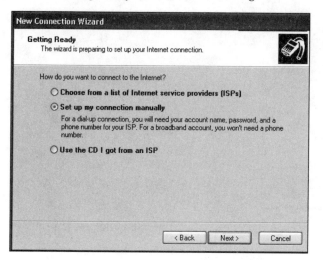

FIGURE 5-2

Telling the Wizard how you want to connect.

4 On the Getting Ready screen, you have three options:

- If you don't already have an account with an ISP, click the Choose From A List Of Internet Service Providers (ISPs) option button, and then click Next. The Wizard will walk you through the process of setting up an account. You'll need a credit card handy in most cases.

- If your ISP provided you with a set-up CD, click the Use The CD I Got From An ISP option button, and then click Next. Click Finish, and then insert the CD in its drive and follow the onscreen instructions.

- If you already have an account with your ISP and were not provided with a set-up CD, click the Set Up My Connection Manually option button, and then click Next to display the Internet Connection screen, shown in Figure 5-3 (next page).

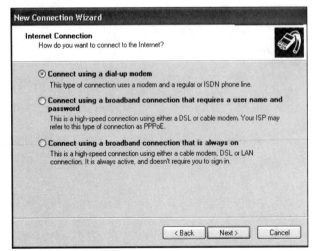

FIGURE 5-3

Telling the Wizard you will connect with a dial-up modem.

5 Click the Connect Using A Dial-Up Modem option button, and then click Next to display the Connection Name screen, as shown in Figure 5-4.

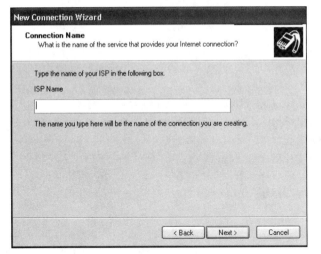

FIGURE 5-4

Enter a name for your connection.

6 In the ISP Name box, enter a name for your connection, and then click Next to display the Phone Number To Dial screen, as shown in Figure 5-5.

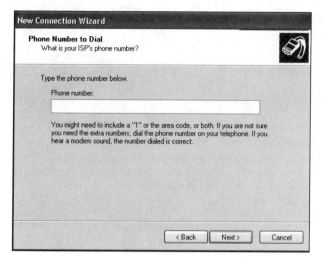

FIGURE 5-5

Enter the phone number of your ISP.

7 In the Phone Number box, enter the dial-up number your ISP provided, and then click Next to display the Internet Account Information screen, as shown in Figure 5-6.

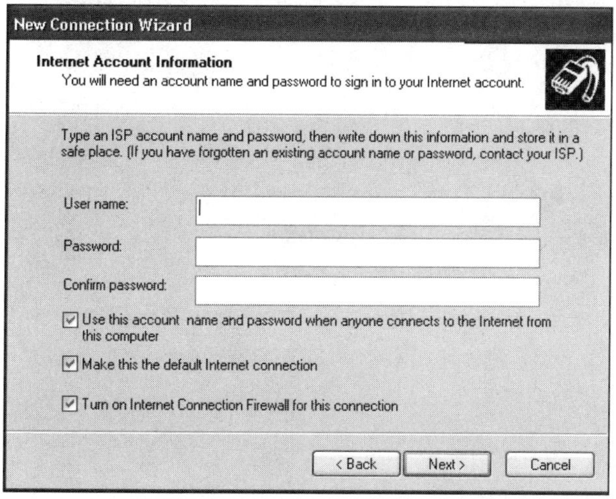

FIGURE 5-6

Providing account information.

8 In the appropriate boxes, enter your user name and your password, and then enter your password again to confirm it. In the bottom part of this screen, you have the following options:

• If you want any person who uses your computer to be able to connect to the Internet using this account, click the first check box.

• If you have more than one Internet connection and want to make this the default connection, click the second check box.

- If you want to enable the firewall that's included with Windows XP, click the third check box.

Note A firewall prevents unauthorized access to your computer from over the Internet. A firewall is not critical when you are connecting with a dial-up modem, but it certainly doesn't hurt anything to enable it. As you will see, if you have a cable modem or a DSL modem, which is always on, you'll absolutely want to enable firewall protection. And if you work on more than a modest two- or three-computer network, you'll want the protection of more robust firewall software that you can acquire from your local computer store or over the Internet.

Note These check boxes are not mutually exclusive. As you can see in Figure 5-6, all can be selected at the same time. When you've entered your account information and made your selections of the check boxes, click Next. On the summary screen, click the Add A Shortcut To The Connection To My Desktop if you want ready access, and then click Finish.

If at any time, you need to change any of the information you supplied during this set-up process, you can run the New Connection Wizard again. To establish specific dialing rules, such as how to access an outside line or dial long distance, or to set up calling card guidelines, you use the Phone and Modem Options applet in Control Panel. Click the Start button, click Control Panel to open Control Panel, click the Printers And Other Hardware link, and then click the Phone And Modem Options link to open the Phone And Modem Options dialog box, shown in Figure 5-7.

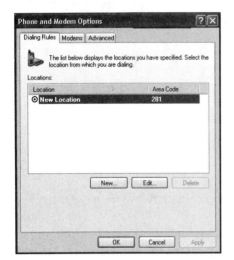

FIGURE 5-7

The Phone And Modem Options dialog box.

If you are having trouble with your modem or want to change some of its settings, such as its speaker volume, you use the Properties dialog box for the modem. Figure 5-8 shows the

Properties dialog box for a modem installed on one of my computers. To open the Properties dialog box for your modem, click the Modems tab in the Phone And Modem Options dialog box, select your modem in the list, and then click the Properties button. You will probably want to consult your ISP before changing some of the more advanced options in this dialog box.

FIGURE 5-8

The Properties dialog box for a modem.

5

Connecting with a Cable Modem

Technically speaking, a cable modem is not really a modem. A modem converts analog signals to digital signals and vice versa. A cable modem transmits and receives only digital signals, but the box that is connected to your cable outlet is popularly referred to as a modem. Information travels through the cable modem to and from your computer over a special channel on your cable signal.

If your cable connection doesn't require you to log on with a user name and password, you don't need to run the New Connection Wizard. If you don't have other firewall protection, though, you should enable Internet Connection Firewall (ICF) that's included with Windows XP. Follow these steps to check that ICF is enabled and to enable it if necessary:

I Click the Start button, click Connect To, and then click Show All Connections to open the Network Connections window, an example of which is shown in Figure 5-9.

FIGURE 5-9

Viewing network connections.

2 Right-click your cable connection, and choose Properties from the shortcut menu to open the Properties dialog box for the connection.

3 Click the Advanced tab, which is shown in Figure 5-10

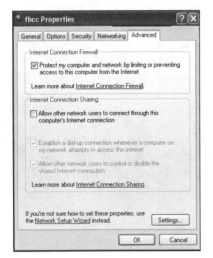

FIGURE 5-10

The Properties dialog box for an Internet connection, open at the Advanced tab.

4 If the first check box is checked, ICF is enabled. If necessary, click this check box, and then click OK to enable ICF.

If you are required to enter a user name and a password for your cable modem connection, you'll need to run the New Connection Wizard. Follow these steps:

1 Click the Start button, click All Programs, click Accessories, click Communications, and then click New Connection Wizard to start the New Connection Wizard.

2 At the Welcome screen, click Next to display the Network Connection Type screen, shown in Figure 5-1 earlier in this chapter.

3 Click the Connect To The Internet option button, and then click Next to display the Getting Ready screen, shown in Figure 5-2 earlier in this chapter.

4 Click the Set Up My Connection Manually option button, and then click Next to display the Internet Connection screen, shown in Figure 5-3 earlier in this chapter.

5 Click the Connect Using A Broadband Connection That Requires A User Name And Password option button, and then click Next to display the Connection Name screen, shown in Figure 5-4.

6 In the ISP name box, enter a name for the connection, and then click Next to open the Internet Account Information screen, shown in Figure 5-6.

7 In the appropriate boxes, enter your user name and your password, and then enter your password again to confirm it. In the bottom part of this screen, you have the following options:

- If you want any person who uses your computer to be able to connect to the Internet using this account, click the first check box.
- If you have more than one Internet connection and want to make this the default connection, click the second check box.
- If you want to enable the firewall that's included with Windows XP, click the third check box.
- These check boxes are not mutually exclusive. As you can see in Figure 5-6, all boxes can be selected at the same time. When you've entered your account information and made your selections of the check boxes, click Next. On the summary screen, click the Add A Shortcut To The Connection To My Desktop if you want ready access, and then click Finish.

Connecting with DSL

If you have a DSL modem and don't have to supply a user name and password to log on, you don't need to run the New Connection Wizard. Remember though that DSL is always on and you'll want some type of firewall protection. If you don't have some other firewall software installed on your system, you'll want to be sure that ICF is enabled as described in the previous section. If you do need to supply a user name and password to log on to your DSL account, run the New Connection Wizard as described in the previous section, giving the Wizard the information it needs about your account.

Depending on your DSL provider and the type of DSL account you have, you may need to take care of some additional configuration as instructed by your provider.

Connecting with ISDN

If you have an ISDN modem that is Plug and Play (and it certainly should be), Windows XP will recognize it and automatically install it during installation of the operating system. You do need to configure it, however. To do so, follow these steps:

1 Click the Start button, click Connect To, and then click Show All Connections to open your Network Connections folder.
2 Right-click your ISDN connection, and choose Properties from the shortcut menu to open the Properties dialog box for your ISDN modem.
3 Click the General tab, select the ISDN device, and then click Configure.
4 In the dialog box that opens, select the type of line you will be using in the Line Type area. If you want to negotiate for a line type, click the Negotiate Line Type check box, and then click OK.

Sharing an Internet Connection

Windows XP includes a feature that allows you to share an Internet connection with other computers on a network. To some extent, though, your ability to do so may depend on whether you have a dial-up connection or a broadband connection, and whether your ISP allows this option. The process varies according to whether you are running Windows XP on all the network computers on your network and the type of Internet connection, so I won't get into all the particulars here. You'll find excellent information in the Windows XP Help and Support Center. To access this information, click the Start button, and then click Help and Support to open the Help and Support Center home page. In the Search box, enter *Internet Connection Sharing*, and press Enter. In the Search Results bar, you'll see a number of topics that will guide your through the process.

Note   Chapter 9 discusses the Help and Support Center in detail. Help and Support Center is a much improved and much more informative and easy-to-use version of Windows Help.

Using E-Mail

E-mail, or electronic mail, is the most popular way to share information over the Internet. Typically, people use e-mail to send and receive little snippets of text: short letters, quick-and-dirty business memos, or personal notes. I have a brother in the Navy, for example, and he's generally unreachable by phone. Regular mail—what e-mail aficionados call snail mail—takes days and days. But I can typically send him an e-mail message and he'll receive it in a few minutes or, in the worst case, in a few hours.

How E-Mail Works

E-mail works like this. You use a program, called an e-mail client, to create your message. Then you tell your e-mail client to send the message to your e-mail post office (which, technically, is called a mail server). Your e-mail post office then sends the message to the recipient's e-mail post office (technically, another mail server). The next time the recipient's e-mail client "visits" the e-mail post office and checks his or her mailbox, the recipient receives the e-mail message.

Before you can send someone an e-mail message, you need to know the person's e-mail name and address. This e-mail name and address identifies both the person you're sending the message to and, in essence, the mail server that the person uses to pick up his or her e-mail messages. This all sounds rather complicated, but an example will show how simple it is.

Note To be picky, you don't actually have to know the name of the recipient's mail server, you only need to know the name of the **domain** of the network of computers the person uses to connect to the Internet.

Suppose you want to send a message to the president of the United States. To do this, you need to know both the domain name that the United States' White House uses for its e-mail, and the e-mail name that the White House uses to identify the president's e-mail. It turns out that the president's full e-mail name and address is president@whitehouse.gov. The president's e-mail name, then, is "president." The White House domain name is "whitehouse.gov". You separate the e-mail name and the domain name with the "@" symbol.

Note When someone verbally gives an e-mail name and address, they say "at" in place of the @ symbol and "dot" in place of the period. So you can also describe the president's e-mail name and address as "president at whitehouse dot gov". Note, however, that the actual e-mail name and address you type is president@whitehouse.gov.

That's really all you need to know to understand and use e-mail. To review, you use e-mail to send and receive messages. To send someone an e-mail message, you need to know the person's e-mail name and address. Figure 5-11 shows a sample e-mail message created using the e-mail client that comes with Windows XP, Outlook Express.

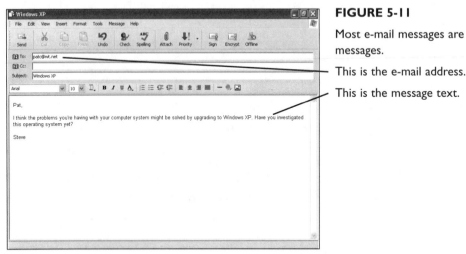

FIGURE 5-11

Most e-mail messages are short text messages.

This is the e-mail address.

This is the message text.

Note In addition to sending text messages, you can also send video, pictures, audio, and Web pages if your system and that of your recipient has this capability. I'll show you how to do so later in this section.

Telling Outlook Express about Your Internet Account

Before you can start sending and receiving messages with Outlook Express, you need to provide Outlook Express with some information about your account. During installation of Windows XP, you may have entered this information, but if you did not or Windows XP was already installed on your computer when you bought it, you'll need to do so now. You'll need the following information from your ISP before you begin this process:

- Your user name and your password.
- The name and type of your incoming mail server.
- The name of your outgoing mail server.
- The name of your ISP's news server if you want to access Internet newsgroups. (I'll explain what newsgroups are and how to access them later in this chapter.)

With this information at hand, follow these steps to set up your Internet account in Outlook Express:

I Click the Start button, and then click Outlook Express to open the main Outlook Express window (see Figure 5-12).

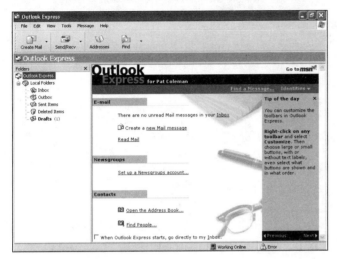

FIGURE 5-12

The main Outlook Express window.

2 Click the Tools menu, and then click Accounts to open the Internet Accounts dialog box (see Figure 5-13).

FIGURE 5-13

The Internet Accounts dialog box.

3 Click the Add button, and then on the submenu click Mail to start the Internet Connection Wizard, as shown in Figure 5-14.

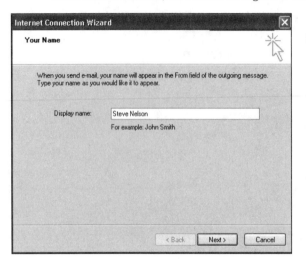

FIGURE 5-14

Starting the Internet Connection Wizard.

4 On the Your Name screen, enter the name that you want to appear in the From field when you send an e-mail message, and then click Next to open the Internet E-mail Address screen, as shown in Figure 5-15.

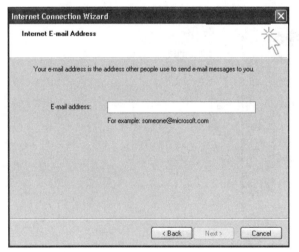

FIGURE 5-15

Enter your e-mail address.

5 Enter your e-mail address, and click Next to open the E-mail Server Names screen, as shown in Figure 5-16.

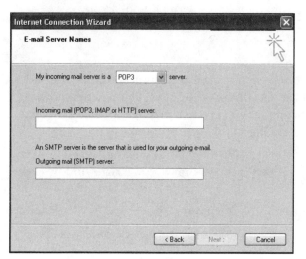

FIGURE 5-16

Enter your e-mail server names.

6 In the My Incoming Mail Server Is A *type* Server, enter the type as provided by your ISP. Click the drop-down list select a type other than POP3. Then in the other boxes enter the names of your incoming and outgoing mail servers. These names will be something like POP3.nelson.com and SMTP.nelson.com. Click Next to open the Internet Mail Logon screen as shown in Figure 5-17.

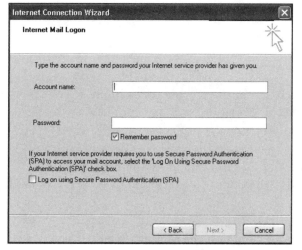

FIGURE 5-17

Enter your account name and password.

7 In the appropriate boxes, enter the account name and password your ISP provided, and then click Next. At the final screen, click Finish. Once you are connected to the Internet, you can now send and receive e-mail messages with Outlook Express.

Creating an E-Mail Message

You can create an e-mail message as plain text or as rich text with all sorts of formatting and bells and whistles such as colors, pictures, and so on. In this section, I'll first describe how to create a plain text message, and then I'll show you how to create a message with fancy effects. To create a plain text e-mail message, follow these steps:

1 Click the Start button, and then click Outlook Express to start Outlook Express.

2 Click the Create Mail toolbar button. Windows displays the New Message window (see Figure 5-18).

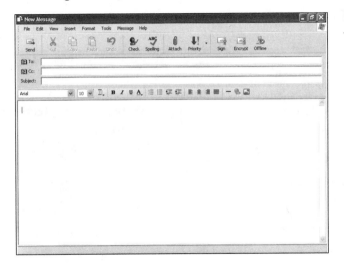

FIGURE 5-18

The empty New Message window.

3 Enter the e-mail name of the message recipient in the To box. For example, if you're sending the president of the United States an e-mail message, type president@white-house.gov in the To box.

4 Optionally, if you want to send a copy of the message to someone else, enter the e-mail name of a message copy recipient in the Cc box. (You can also select recipients from your Address Box once you have entered their contact information. I'll show you how later in this chapter.)

Note You can send a message and message copy to more than one recipient. To do this, enter multiple e-mail names separated by semicolons.

---

5 Type a brief description of your message's subject in the Subject box.

6 Type your message in the message area beneath the Message window's Formatting toolbar. Figure 5-19 shows a message.

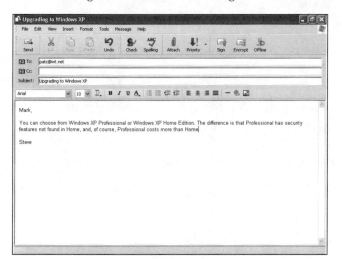

FIGURE 5-19

A message ready to be sent.

7 Click the Send toolbar button to send your message. By default, Outlook Express sends your message immediately if you are connected to the Internet. If you are not connected to the Internet, your message is placed in your Outbox folder, where it stays until you are connected. You can change how messages are sent by selecting settings in the Options dialog box in Outlook Express, and later in this chapter I'll show you how to do this and customize Outlook Express in other ways.

Note   If any Microsoft Office program that includes a spelling checker is installed on your system, you'll see the Spelling button in the New Message window. Especially in a business setting, it's a good idea to spell check your messages before sending them on their way.

If your recipient's e-mail program understands how to display any formatting you apply, you can send that person a rich text e-mail message. The message then, in essence, becomes a Web page because Outlook Express formats it using HTML (HyperText Markup Language), the language use to create Web pages that can be displayed in a Web browser. Before you send messages formatted in HTML, you need to find out if your recipient's e-mail program can display them. The simplest way to do this is to send them a plain text message and ask.

To compose a message in HTML, you use the tools on the Formatting bar (see Figure 5-20) in the New Message window.

FIGURE 5-20

The Formatting bar.

Note   If the Formatting toolbar is grayed out, click the Format menu, and then click Rich Text (HTML). Now click in the body of the message.

You use the tools on the Formatting bar, in order from left to right, to do the following:

- Click the Font drop-down list to select a font for what you type. (For information about fonts, look back at Chapter 4.)
- Click the Font Size drop-down list to choose a size for the selected font.
- Click the Paragraph Style drop-down list to see a selection of ways you can format a paragraph.
- Click the Bold button to boldface selected text.
- Click the Italic button to italicize selected text.
- Click the Underline button to underline selected text.
- Click the Font Color button to display a drop-down list of colors that you can apply to selected text.
- Click the Formatting Numbers button to format text you type as a numbered list.
- Click the Formatting Bullets button to format text you type as a bulleted list.
- Click the Decrease Indentation button to reduce the size of the left margin.
- Click the Increase Indentation button to enlarge the size of the left margin.
- Click the Align Left button to align the text of a paragraph with the left margin. The right margin will be ragged (uneven).
- Click the Center button to center each line of a paragraph.
- Click the Align Right button to align the text of a paragraph with the right margin. The left margin will be ragged (uneven).
- Click the Justify button to align the text of a paragraph with both the left and the right margins.
- Click the Insert Horizontal Line button to add a horizontal line at the insertion point.
- Type an e-mail address or a Web address, select it, and then click the Create A Hyperlink button to open the Hyperlink dialog box and format the selection as a hyperlink.
- Click the Insert Picture button to open the Picture dialog box, which you can use to locate and insert a picture and, if you want, some alternate text in a message.

Figure 5-21 shows a message that was created using some of the tools on the Formatting tool-bar.

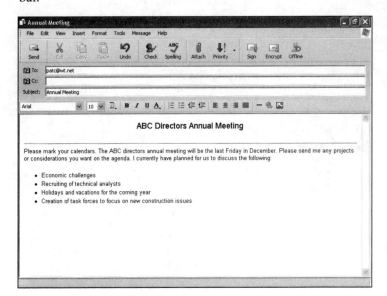

FIGURE 5-21

A message formatted as rich text.

Delivering E-Mail Messages

To deliver the messages in your Outbox folder to your outgoing mail server, click the Send/Recv toolbar button or choose the Tools menu's Send And Receive command. If your computer isn't currently connected to the Internet, Windows makes the connection. Then Windows delivers your outgoing messages and retrieves any incoming messages.

Reading E-Mail Messages

To read your e-mail messages, click the Inbox folder. Outlook Express lists your messages in the Folder Contents pane and shows a message in the Preview pane (see Figure 5-22 on the next page).

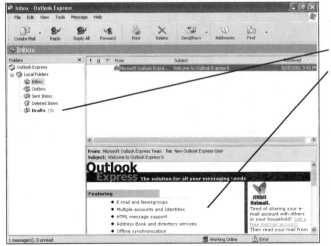

If you want to open a new window especially for a message—perhaps so that you can see more of the message—double-click the message in the Folder Contents pane. Outlook Express opens a window for the message.

Deleting Messages from Your Inbox

To delete a message in one of the Outlook Express folders, select it and then press the Delete key or click the Delete toolbar button. You can also right-click the message and choose the shortcut menu's Delete command.

When you delete a message, Outlook Express moves the message to the Deleted Items folder. If you erroneously delete a message, you can still restore it. To restore a message, follow these steps:

1 Click the Deleted Items folder icon. Outlook Express opens the folder and displays its contents in the Folder Contents pane.

2 Click the message you want to restore, and then drag it to a folder—to your Inbox folder for example.

Because every message you delete actually gets moved to the Deleted Items folder, the number of messages stored in this folder grows quickly. To empty the Deleted Items folder, follow these steps:

1 Right-click the Deleted Items folder.

2 Choose the shortcut menu's Empty 'Deleted Items' Folder command.

Once you delete a message from the Deleted Items folder or empty the Deleted Items folder, the message is permanently lost.

Note In the later section "Customizing Outlook Express," I'll show you other ways to deal with messages in the Deleted Items folder.

Replying to E-Mail Messages

You can send a reply message to someone who's sent you a message. To reply to a message, follow these steps:

1 Open the message.

2 Click the Reply toolbar button. Outlook Express creates a new message for you, filling in the To box with the e-mail name and address of the person you're replying to (see Figure 5-23). Outlook Express also fills in the Subject box for you and then copies the original message text.

3 Add any new text to the message.

4 Delete any unneeded text from the original message text.

5 Click the Send toolbar button.

6 Deliver the message in the usual way.

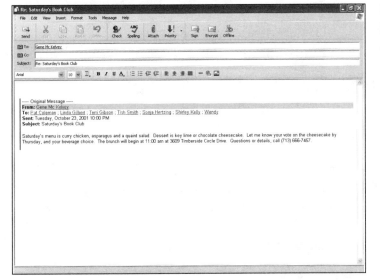

FIGURE 5-23

Reply to messages you receive by clicking the Reply toolbar button.

You can reply to a message and send a copy of your reply to every recipient of the original message by clicking the Reply All toolbar button.

Forwarding an E-Mail Message

You can easily forward a copy of any message you receive to someone else. To forward a message, follow these steps:

1 Open the message.

2 Click the Forward toolbar button. Outlook Express creates a new message for you, filling in the Subject box and then copying the original message text.

3 Enter the e-mail name and address of the message recipient in the To box.

4 Add any new text to the message.

5 Click the Send toolbar button.

6 Deliver the message in the usual way.

E-Mailing a File Attachment

You can easily e-mail files using Outlook Express, and these files can be text, pictures, audio, video, and so on. When you e-mail a file, you simply attach a copy of the file to the message.

To e-mail a file attachment, follow these steps:

1 Click the Create Mail toolbar button to open the New Message window.

2 Enter the e-mail name of the message recipient in the To box.

3 To send a copy of the message to someone else, enter the e-mail name of a message copy recipient in the Cc box.

4 Type a brief description of your message's subject in the Subject box.

5 Type your message in the message area. (If you're composing a formatted message, the message area is the area beneath the Formatting toolbar.)

6 Click the Insert menu, and then click the File Attachment command to open the Insert Attachment dialog box (see Figure 5-24).

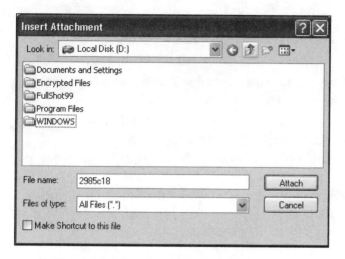

FIGURE 5-24

The Insert Attachment dialog box.

7 Use the Look In list box to identify the disk and folder holding the file you want to attach.

8 Double-click the file you want to attach to the message. Outlook Express attaches the file to the message, as shown in Figure 5-25.

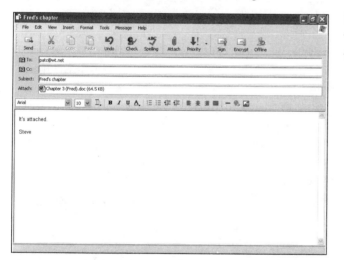

FIGURE 5-25

The New Message window with message text and a file attachment.

If you are attaching a large file such as a photo or a number of photos, you'll want to compress them (make them smaller) so that they transmit faster. Windows XP includes a compression feature that lets you easily compress files in Outlook Express. (I showed you how to use this feature in the My Computer folder in Chapter 3.) Your recipient can easily uncompress the file and view it, even if they are not using Windows XP. To compress a file you are attaching to an e-mail message, follow these steps:

1 In the Insert Attachment dialog box, right-click the file you want to compress, choose Send To from the shortcut menu, and then choose Compressed Folder.

2 Double-click the compressed folder (it has a zipper) to attach the file to your message.

To select multiple files to compress, hold down the Ctrl key and select each one. Now right-click the selection, click Send To, and click Compressed Folder.

If you receive a message with a file attachment, you can detach the file attachment from the message and permanently save the attachment. To do this, follow these steps:

1 Double-click the message header in the Folder Contents pane to display the message in its own window.

2 Click the File menu, and then click Save Attachments to open the Save Attachments dialog box.

3 Name the file and specify in which folder it should be saved.

Note   For more information about how to save files, refer to Chapter 3, "Files, Folders, and Disks."

Note   If you want to only open a file attachment—not save it—you can do so by double-clicking its icon.

Creating and Using an Address Book

If you send and receive a lot of e-mail (and that's most of us these days), you'll want to create contact information in Address Book. Address Book is a Windows XP accessory, and you'll see an icon for it (called Addresses) on the toolbar in the main Outlook Express window. You can add a name, e-mail address, and other contact information about a person in a several ways.

To add a person's e-mail name and address to your Address Book if you've received a message from the person, right-click the message header in the Folder Contents pane, and choose Add Sender To Address Book from the shortcut menu.

If you always want to place the names of people your reply to in your Address Book, follow these steps:

1 Click the Tools menu, and then click Options to open the Options dialog box, as shown in Figure 5-26.

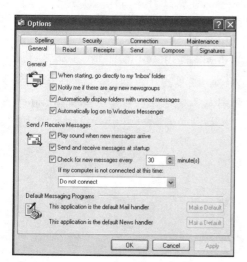

FIGURE 5-26

The Options dialog box.

2 Click the Send tab, which is shown in Figure 5-27.

FIGURE 5-27

The Options dialog box, open at the Send tab.

3 Click the Automatically Put People I Reply To In My Address Book, and then click OK.

Note In the later section, "Customizing Outlook Express," I'll show you how to use the Options dialog box to adjust other features of Outlook Express.

To add a person's e-mail name and address and other contact information to your Address Book if you haven't received a message from the person, follow these steps:

I Click the Addresses toolbar button to open Address Book, as shown in Figure 5-28.

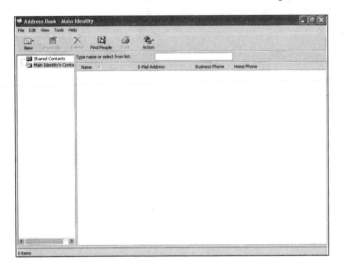

2 Click the New button, and then click New Contact to open the Properties dialog box shown in Figure 5-29.

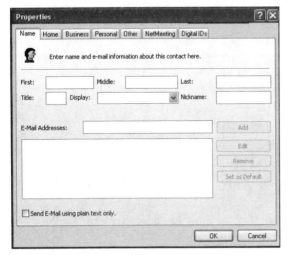

3 Use the text boxes to record a person's name information, and then enter the person's e-mail address in the E-Mail Addresses text box. If the person has more than one e-mail address, enter a name and press Add for the first address. The e-mail address appears in the box below. Now enter any other addresses, pressing Add after each addition. To

specify one e-mail address as the default (the one you always use when sending mail to this person), select it, and then click Set As Default.

4 On the other tabs of the Properties dialog box, enter as much or as little information as you want to maintain about this person. Click the tab, and then press Tab to move from field to field on a tab.

5 When you have finished entering information, click the OK button. Address Book now shows the new name.

To use a name you've entered in Address Book, follow these steps:

1 With the New Message window displayed, click the card icon next to the To box. Outlook Express displays the Select Recipients dialog box, as shown in Figure 5-30.

Note As long as a recipient's name is in the Address Book, you can enter it in the To box simply by typing the first couple of letters in the name. If Outlook Express recognizes the name, it enters the name for you.

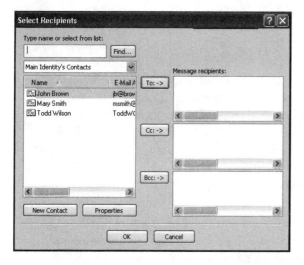

FIGURE 5-30

The Select Recipients dialog box shows the e-mail names and addresses you've collected.

2 To add a name to the To box, click the name to select it and then click the To button.

3 To add a name to the Cc box, click the name to select it and then click the Cc button.

4 To add a name to the Bcc box, click the name to select it and then click the Bcc button.

5 Click the OK button when you've finished collecting names from the Address Book. Then create your message in the usual way.

Working with Newsgroups

Newsgroups represent another way to share information over the Internet. In essence, a newsgroup works like a bulletin board that people use to post e-mail messages. Other people then read these messages. Typically, you use your e-mail client program to post and read the messages posted on a newsgroup bulletin board.

Because there are hundreds of thousands of people who post messages on thousands of different topics and millions of people who want to read these messages, each newsgroup contains only those messages that fall into a specific category. For example, there's a newsgroup for people interested in the music of guitarist Steve Vai. There's a newsgroup for people interested in brewing beer. There's a newsgroup for people interested in Disneyland trivia. And as you might expect, there are hundreds and hundreds of newsgroups for specialty computer topics.

Note   Much of the Internet's sexual content that you hear about is available through newsgroups. In fact, two of the Internet's most popular newsgroups, alt.binaries.pictures.erotica and alt.stories.sex, provide sexually explicit material. But be aware that most newsgroups are not censored and that you can find anything almost anywhere.

Setting Up a Newsgroup Account

As I mentioned earlier in this chapter, you have to give Outlook Express some information about your Internet account before you can send and receive e-mail. You also need to give Outlook Express some information before you can read or post messages to newsgroups. Primarily, you need the name of your ISP's news server. During the installation of Windows XP, you may have been given the opportunity to provide this information. If you chose not to do so at that time or if you bought a new computer that already had Windows XP installed on it, you'll need to do so now. Follow these steps:

1. In the main Outlook Express window, click the Set Up A Newsgroups Account link to start the Internet Connection Wizard, which opens at the Your Name screen.

2. Enter the name that you want to appear when you post a message to a newsgroup. Many people prefer anonymity when accessing newsgroups. You can enter either your real name or an alias. Click Next to open the Internet New E-mail Address screen.

3. Enter your e-mail address and click Next. Again, many people prefer not to use their real e-mail address but a fake one for security purposes. If you want to enter a fake address, you might want to first check with your ISP. Some ISPs have rules about this.

4. On the Internet News Server Name screen, shown in Figure 5-31, enter the name of the news server as supplied by your ISP. This name will be something like news.xyz.net. Click Next.

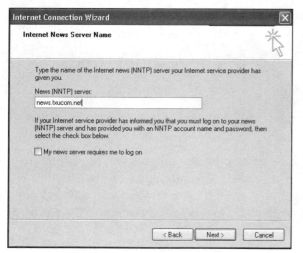

FIGURE 5-31

Enter the name of your news server.

5 Click Finish. Outlook Express now displays a message box asking if you would like to download the list of newsgroups for the news account you just added. To do so click Yes.

When the list has downloaded (only the names are downloaded, not the content), you'll see the Newsgroup Subscriptions dialog box, shown in Figure 5-32.

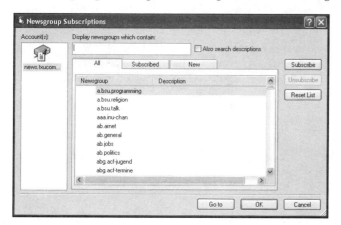

FIGURE 5-32

The Newsgroup Subscriptions dialog box.

Reading Newsgroup Messages

You can select a newsgroup to read by scrolling this list (a time-consuming task) or by searching on a term. To search, enter a term in the Display Newsgroups Which Contain box, and then simply wait. Soon you'll see a list of newsgroups whose names contain the search term. To read a newsgroup, select it and then click Go To. If you find a group that seems to have value for you, you can subscribe to it. Subscribing simply means creating a subfolder for a particular newsgroup in your news folder

When you open a newsgroup by clicking Go To, a list of messages posted to this group opens in Outlook Express. Click a subject line in the top pane to open the message in the lower pane. Or double-click the subject line to open the message in its own window.

Posting to a Newsgroup

Relaying to a newsgroup article or sending a message to a newsgroup is known as *posting*. To send an original message to a newsgroup, open the newsgroup and then click the New Post button. The New Message window will open with the group's name in the To line. To reply via e-mail to the author of a post, click the Reply button; to reply via a posting to the entire newsgroup, click the Reply Group button.

Note   If you post messages to newsgroups, you tend to receive lots of unsolicited e-mail from people who want to sell you various products and services—including many products or services that you may find offensive.

Customizing Outlook Express

You can customize Outlook Express in many, many ways, and I'm not going to describe all of them here by any means. I do want to show you how to make some changes that I mentioned earlier in this chapter as well as how to customize some other items that are rather basic to using Outlook Express. You take care of any customizations in the Options dialog box. In the main Outlook Express window, click Tools and then click Options to open the Options dialog box. Figure 5-33 shows this dialog box open at the General tab. In this section I'm not going to discuss all these tabs or all the options on a tab, but I will point out what I think are some of the more important options you can set for basic use of Outlook Express.

FIGURE 5-33

The Options dialog box open at the General tab.

Here are some items you'll probably want to customize on the General tab:

- If you want to display your Inbox when you start Outlook Express instead of the Outlook Express main window, click the When Starting, Go Directly To My 'Inbox' folder.

- If you want to hear a sound when new messages arrive, click the Play Sound When New Messages Arrive check box. For example, you have opened Outlook Express and minimized it but you are still connected to the Internet. You go about your business of entering data in a spreadsheet or another application. If you get new mail, you'll hear the sound and then can decided whether to stop and check e-mail or wait until later.

- When you are connected to the Internet, you can specify that Outlook Express automatically check for new mail periodically. To do so, click the Check For New Messages Every *x* Minute(s) check box, and then specify a number of minutes in the spin box.

Here are some items you'll probably want to customize on the Send tab, which is shown in Figure 5-34:

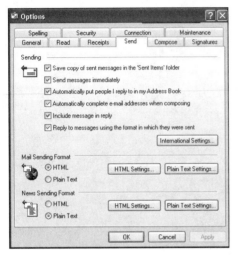

FIGURE 5-34

The Options dialog box open at the Send tab.

- If you want to retain a copy of all the messages you send, click the Save Copy Of Sent Messages In The 'Sent' Folder check box. If you send and receive a lot of business messages, you'll want to be sure this check box is selected. An e-mail trail can be just as vital as a paper trail.

- If you want to send messages immediately when you click the Send/Recv button, click the Send Messages Immediately button. When you are connected to the Internet and this check box is selected, you bypass the Outbox folder.

- When you reply to an e-mail message, it is often convenient and sometimes necessary to include the text of the original message. This happens automatically when the Include Message In Reply check box is selected. However, I need to mention that, by convention, always including the original message in a reply is somewhat frowned upon because it squanders bandwidth. That is, it takes longer for an e-mail message to travel to its destination. In these days of broadband connections, this is really not an issue, but it was in early modem days. Unfortunately, there's no way to selectively choose to include the original message in a reply. This feature is either of or on. What you can do, however, is leave this check box selected; then if you don't want to include the original message, in the reply window move the insertion point to the body of the message, click the Edit menu, and then press Delete.

- Be sure that the Reply To Messages Using The Format In Which They Were Sent check box is selected. In this way, you won't send a message formatted as rich text to someone whose e-mail program can't display it properly.

Figure 5-35 shows the Maintenance tab of the Options tab. I'll point out only one item here, and that is the Empty Messages From The 'Deleted' Items Folder On Exit check box. If you're rather sure that you truly want to dispose of any item you delete, setting this option prevents your Deleted Items folder from getting packed with deleted messages. Every time you close Outlook Express, the Deleted Items folder is emptied automatically.

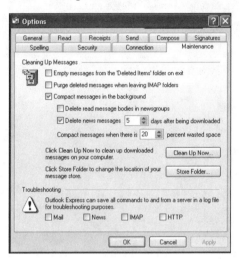

FIGURE 5-35

The Options dialog box, open at the Maintenance tab.

Instant Messaging with Windows Messenger

Instant messaging is a hot component of Internet communications these days, and Windows Messenger is an instant messaging program in Windows XP that lets you do the following—all in real time:

- Chat online
- Add voice to an online conversation
- Add video to an online conversation
- Transfer files

In this section, I'm not going to be able to tell you everything there is to know about Windows Messenger, but I will tell you how to get started, how to add people to your list of contacts, and how to send and receive instant messages. For information on configuring Windows Messenger for voice, audio, and other features, click Help in Windows Messenger.

To start Windows Messenger, click the Start button, click All Programs, and then click Windows Messenger. Before you can actually use Windows Messenger, you must have a .NET Passport, as will all your contacts with whom you will eventually communicate, and all your contacts must be using Windows Messenger. If you don't have a .NET Passport, Windows Messenger displays a Click Here To Sign In link in its window the first time you open

Windows Messenger. Click this link to start the .NET Passport Wizard, which will step you through the process. Once you have a .NET Passport, Windows Messenger signs you in, and you'll see the screen shown in Figure 5-36.

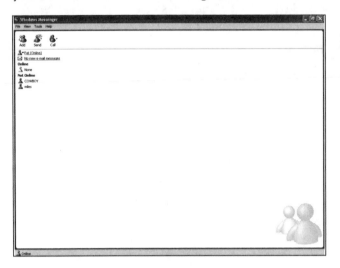

FIGURE 5-36

Starting Windows Messenger.

Adding Contacts

Before you can chat or communicate in any other way with Windows Messenger, you need to create your contacts list. Obviously, this list is empty if you've just opened Windows Messenger for the first time and signed on. To add a contact if you know the person's e-mail address, follow these steps:

I In the Windows Messenger window, click Add to open the Add A Contact dialog box, which is shown in Figure 5-37.

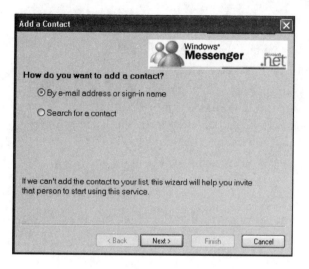

FIGURE 5-37

The Add A Contact dialog box.

2 Click the By E-Mail Address Or Sign-In Name option, and then click Next.

3 Enter the complete e-mail address in the text box, and then click Next.

4 If the contact you want to add does not have a .NET Passport, they will need to get one. Windows Messenger offers to send your contact a message that explains the process. You can add your own comments to this message. If you want to do this, click Next.

5 Red the message that Windows Messenger will send, add a comment if you want, and then click Finish.

If you don't know the e-mail address of the contact you want to add, follow these steps:

1 In the Add A Contact dialog box, click the Search For A Contact option, and then click Next.

2 Enter your contact's first and last names in the appropriate check boxes and location information. You can now search the Hotmail Member Directory or your own Address Book for the e-mail address by clicking the Search For The Person At drop-down list box. Make a selection, and click Next.

3 If Windows Messenger locates the address, it will appear in the Search Results screen. Select it and click Next.

4 If the person you want to add to the list has not given permission to be added, Windows Messenger will offer to send them a message, asking them to contact you.

Sending an Instant Message

To send an instant message to someone on your contact list, follow these steps:

1 Double-click your contact to open the Instant Message window.

2 In the lower part of the window, type your message. If you are sending a message to a person at another computer, your message can be a maximum of 400 characters. If you are sending a message to a person who is using a mobile device such as a cell phone, your message can be a maximum of about 160 characters.

3 Click the Send button to send your message. Your message will be sent, and it will appear in the upper part of the window. Any message you receive will also appear in the upper part of the window.

The status bar of the Instant Message window will show you when the other person is typing and the date and time of the last message you received.

Chapter 6

Sharing Information Over the Internet

Microsoft Windows XP doesn't distinguish between the files you've stored on a local disk, a network disk, or the files stored on the Internet. You can—for all practical purposes—grab a document from just about anywhere in the same basic way. And this means that Windows gives you easy access to a sea of information. The tool you use to access this sea of information is called a web browser. This chapter looks at how to use Internet Explorer, the web browser that's included with Windows XP.

In particular, this chapter talks about the following topics:

- Using the Internet Explorer window
- Saving and printing web pages
- Searching the Internet
- Customizing Internet Explorer

> **Note** This chapter assumes that you've already connected to the Internet. If you have questions about how you do this, please refer to Chapter 5, "Communicating on the Internet." That chapter begins by talking about how you connect to the Internet.

Opening Internet Explorer

You can open Internet Explorer in several ways:

- Click the Start button, and then click Internet Explorer.
- Click the Start button, click All Programs, and then click Internet Explorer.
- If the Quick Launch bar is displayed on the Taskbar, click the Launch Internet Explorer Browser icon.
- If an Internet Explorer shortcut appears on the desktop, click the shortcut.

In addition, if a web page address appears in an e-mail message or another document, you can click the address to open that page in Internet Explorer. Also, in Windows Explorer, if you click a filename that has the .htm or .html extension, that file will open in Internet Explorer.

Note Web page addresses are also known by the term Uniform Resource Locator, or URL.

The first time you open Internet Explorer after installing Windows XP, you'll see the Web page shown in Figure 6-1. You can instead choose to display another Web page as your home or a blank page. I'll show you how in the later section "Customizing Internet Explorer."

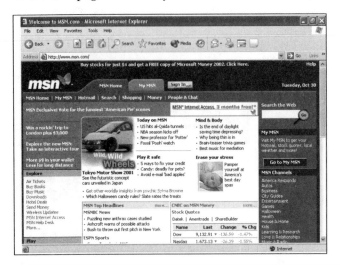

FIGURE 6-1

The default home page in Internet Explorer.

Note If you bought your computer with Windows XP already installed on it, you may see some other start page—for example, the home page of the computer manufacturer.

The components of the Internet Explorer window are similar to those in other Windows XP windows. Vertical and horizontal scroll bars appear as necessary, and you can size portions of the window by clicking and dragging. When you point to a button, you'll see a ScreenTip that tells you what the button does. Here are some other components:

- At the very top of the window is the title bar, which displays the name of the current web page or other open file.
- Just beneath the title bar is the menu bar, which contains a set of menus. You'll notice that many of these also appear in other Windows applications.
- Just beneath the menu bar is the Standard toolbar. It contains several buttons that correspond to items on the menu bar, as well as Back and Forward buttons and the Home button.
- Just beneath the Standard toolbar is the Address bar. You use it to enter a URL or a filename.
- The Links bar is a drop-down list on the far right of the Address bar. It contains a short list of preselected hyperlinks. You can add or remove links from this list.

- At the far right of the menu bar is the Activity Indicator. When Internet Explorer is sending or receiving data, the Activity Indicator is animated.
- The main window displays the resource you most recently accessed.
- The status bar is at the bottom of the screen. When you choose a menu command, the status bar displays a description of what it does. When you point to a link, the status bar displays the URL. When you click a link, the status bar displays a series of messages about the progress of finding and opening that resource.
- The security zone indicator is at the far right of the status bar and displays the currently active security zone. I'll explain security zones in the section "Customizing Internet Explorer."

Another component of the Internet Explorer window is called an Explorer bar. An Explorer bar is displayed in a pane to the left of the main window. Examples of the Explorer bar are the Search Companion and the Favorites bar. I'll explain both of these bars later in this chapter.

Using Internet Explorer Features

Version 6 of Internet Explorer is included with Windows XP. If you've worked with Internet Explorer before, you'll see that version 6 contains several classic features, drops some features that were in some previous versions, and adds new features.

Using the Address Bar

Before I get into how to use the Address bar, I need to explain a bit more about web addresses, also called, as I mentioned earlier, URLs. As an example, take a look at Figure 6-2 (next page), the home page of the White House. The address shown in the Address bar is *http://www.whitehouse.gov*. The *http://* part of this address is the code, or protocol, that identifies the address as a World Wide Web page. The *www* indicates that the resource is on the World Wide Web, *whitehouse* is the server, and *.gov* is the domain name. This address actually represents a string of numbers called an Internet Protocol (IP) address, for example, 169.254.69.104. Since it's much easier for humans to remember names instead of numbers, we typically use URLs. When you're communicating a URL orally, you pronounce the period in the address as "dot."

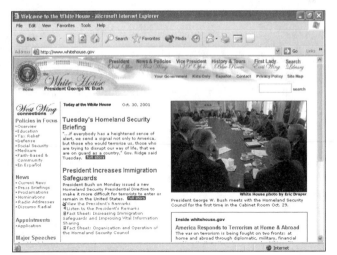

FIGURE 6-2

The home page of the White House.

To open a resource on the World Wide Web when you know its address, you enter the address in the Address bar and then press Enter. But you don't always have to enter the entire address. If you've entered the URL previously, it may sort of complete itself after you've entered a few characters. This is the AutoComplete feature at work. You also don't need to enter the *hppt://* part of the address. Internet Explorer assumes that the address you are entering begins with this protocol. Of course, if you are entering an address that begins with another protocol, such as *ftp,* you'll need to enter that protocol.

Note Here's a handy trick you can use to go to a Web site that beings with www and ends with com. All you need to do is enter the main part of the name. For example, to go to http://www.microsoft.com, simply enter "microsoft" and press Enter.

There are many other ways to access Web sites, though, than using the Address bar, and you'll see them as you work through the rest of this chapter.

Following Hyperlinks

The Web consists of multimedia documents, or web pages, connected by hyperlinks. A multimedia document is a document that uses multiple media for communicating information. For example, text is one medium. Pictures are another. Sound is still another. So multimedia documents are documents that use text, pictures, and sometimes even sound.

The unique feature of web documents is that they also include hyperlinks. A hyperlink, essentially, is an address that points to another web page. When you click a hyperlink, you're actually telling Windows to retrieve and then display the web document identified by the hyperlink. If you click a hyperlink, Windows retrieves a different web document. For example, clicking the hyperlink "5 ways to fix your credit" in Figure 6-1 takes you to the page shown in Figure 6-3.

FIGURE 6-3

The page that results from clicking a hyperlink.

A hyperlink can be a word, a phrase, an image, or a symbol, and its target can be located on your local computer, your local network, or the Internet. Textual links are usually underlined and in a different color from normal text. You know something is a hyperlink if the pointer becomes a hand with a pointing finger when you place the mouse cursor over it.

If you ever lose track of where you are when following links, click Home to return to your start page. Click Back to return to the page you last visited, or click Forward to return to the page that you visited before you clicked the Back button.

Accessing Favorite Sites

Another way to keep track of sites that you visit often or want to return to is to add them to your Favorites list. (In some web browsers, such as Netscape Navigator, favorites are called bookmarks.) When a site is on the Favorites list, you can simply click it to go there rather than typing its address in the Address bar.

You can add sites to your Favorites list in two ways: by using the Favorites menu, and by clicking the Favorites button on the toolbar. To use the Favorites menu, follow these steps:

1 Open the page that you want to add.

2 Click the Favorites menu, and then click Add To Favorites to open the Add Favorite dialog box, which is shown in Figure 6-4.

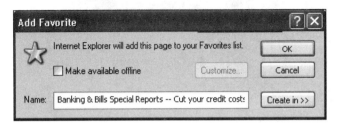

FIGURE 6-4

The Add Favorite dialog box.

3 In the Name box, accept the suggested name, or type another name and then click OK to add the site to your list.

To use the Favorites toolbar button, click it to open the Favorites bar, as shown in Figure 6-5. Click Add to open the Add Favorite dialog box, and the follow steps 2 and 3 above.

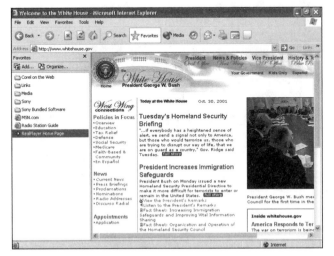

FIGURE 6-5

Using the Favorites bar to add a favorite site.

Here are some other ways to add a site to your Favorites list:

- Right-click a link, and choose Add To Favorites from the shortcut menu.
- Right-click the current pages outside a link, and choose Add To Favorites from the shortcut menu.
- Drag and drop a link on a web page to the Favorites toolbar button.

Using the History Bar

Another great way to find a page you've visited and want to revisit is to locate it on the History bar. Internet Explorer keeps track of all the sites you've visited in previous days and weeks, and you can view them in several ways. To open the History bar, click the History button on the toolbar. Figure 6-6 shows the History bar.

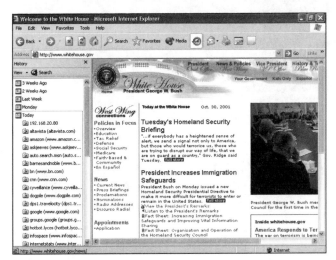

FIGURE 6-6

Using the History bar in Internet Explorer.

To select how you want to view the sites listed in the History bar, click the View button to display the drop-down list. You can display sites by date, site, most visited, or most visited today. You can also open a list of sites that you visited during a certain past time period. If you remember some key word or phrase in the site's title, you can search the history list for it. Click the Search button, and then in the Search For box, type a word or phrase, and click Search Now.

Note If you often visit a site and want quick access to it but don't want to make it your start page, place a shortcut to it on your desktop. With the page open in Internet Explorer, right-click an empty area of the page, and then choose Create Shortcut from the shortcut menu.

Using the Media Bar

The Media bar is a feature of Internet Explorer that you can use to play music, videos, or multimedia files and listen to Internet radio stations. The Media bar is a subset of Windows Media Player (see Chapter 11) and has the same controls as Media Player at the bottom of the bar. To open the Media bar, click the Media button on the Standard toolbar. Figure 6-7 shows the beginning of a movie preview.

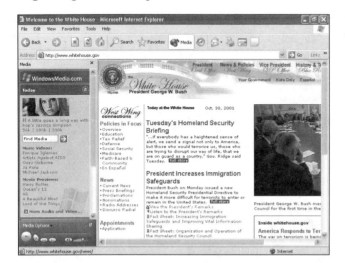

FIGURE 6-7

The Media bar in Internet Explorer.

To see what a control does, simply point to it. You use the Media bar features as follows:

- Click a link in the Featured Artists section to open a page for that item. You can then click a link corresponding to the speed of your Internet connection to play the item.
- Click a link in the Movie Previews to open a preview and play it.
- Click a link in the Radio Stations section to open that station's page and listen to what's playing.
- Click a link on the side of the Media bar to display more selections.

Note   You'll find that you need a fast Internet connection to use the Media bar items satisfactorily. Although at least a 56-Kbps modem is the minimum recommended standard, this speed is not really acceptable for most purposes.

Saving and Printing Web Pages

Although the World Wide Web is an incredibly dynamic environment, you will sometimes run across a web page that contains information that is for the most part not going to change. If you want ready access to the page, you can save it as a file to a local drive or to a drive on your network. I occasionally find this handy for quick access to government reports and the like.

To save a Web page that is open in Internet Explorer, follow these steps:

1 Click the File menu, and then click Save As to open the Save Web Page dialog box, which is shown in Figure 6-8.

FIGURE 6-8

The Save Web Page dialog box.

2 In the Save In box, select a folder in which to save the page. In the File Name box, accept the name that's suggested or enter another name. In the Save As Type box, select a file type.

3 Click the Save button to save the page as a file.

To save a Web page without opening it, right-click its hyperlink and choose Save Target As from the shortcut menu to download the file and open the Save As dialog box. Follow steps 2 and 3 above.

To save a portion of a page and place it in another document, follow these steps:

1 Select what you want to save, and then press Ctrl+C.

2 Open the document in which you want to place the selection, place the insertion point where you want the selection, and press Ctrl+V.

To save an image from a Web page, follow these steps:

 1 Right-click the image, and choose Save Picture As to open the Save Picture dialog box, as shown in Figure 6-9.

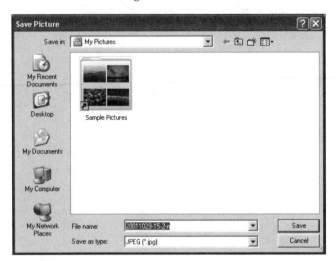

FIGURE 6-9

The Save Picture dialog box.

 2 Select a folder, a filename, and a type, and then click Save.

Printing in Internet Explorer is similar to printing in any other Windows application. Simply click the Print button on the toolbar to print a page with the default settings for your printer. By default, background colors and background images are not printed, which save printing time, spooling time, and cartridge ink. If you do want to print background colors and images, follow these steps:

 1 Click the Tools menu, click Internet Options to open the Internet Options dialog box, and then click the Advanced tab, which is shown in Figure 6-10.

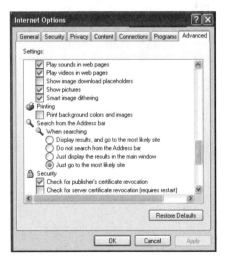

FIGURE 6-10

The Internet Options dialog box, open at the Advanced tab.

Note   Later in this chapter, I'll discuss how to use the Internet Options dialog box to customize
        Internet Explorer in other ways.

2   Scroll down the Settings list, and in the Printing section, click the Print Background
    Colors And Images check box. Click OK.

To print a web page but to exercise finer control over what's printed, such as the number of
copies, follow these steps:

1   Click the File menu, and then click Print to open the Print dialog box.

Note   For more information about using the Print dialog box, look back at Chapter 4.

2   Click the Options tab, as shown in Figure 6-11. If you want to print all the pages that
    are linked to the current page, click the Print All Linked Documents check box. (Be sure
    you really want to do this; you might need a lot of paper.) If you want to print a table
    that lists the links for this page, click the Print Table Of Links check box.

FIGURE 6-11

The Print dialog box, open at the Options tab.

6

3   Click the Print button to begin printing the page.

Sometimes a web page will offer you the opportunity to view and print the page in a format
that is specifically for printing purposes. Usually, this page is a text-only format that you
reach by clicking a button or a link that says something such as "Print Version." This format
is particularly useful for printing items such as recipes, reports, and the like.

Searching the Internet

No one knows for sure, of course, but it is reasonable to estimate that there are billions of publicly available pages on the Internet. Consequently, it is unlikely that you'll simply happen on to information that is exactly what you need. Fortunately, many excellent tools are available to help you search. In the first part of this section, I'll show you how to use the tools in Internet Explorer to search the Internet, and then I'll point you to some other search services that are useful for finding particular categories of information.

Doing a Simple Search

Before I get into how you use the Search Companion bar, which is the primary Internet Explorer search tool, I want to tell you about a very simple way to search on a word or phrase: simply type it in the Address bar and press Enter. If this seems too easy, just try it. Figure 6-12 shows the results I got when I searched on the phrase "Internet statistics." To open a page, simply click its link.

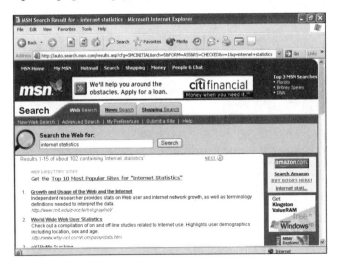

FIGURE 6-12

The results of searching from the Address bar.

Widening the Search

When you search from the Address bar, you're using MSN Search, but if you search using the Search Companion bar, you have the opportunity to use other Internet search services as well. To see how this works, follow these steps:

1. Click the Search button on the toolbar to open the Search Companion bar, which is shown in Figure 6-13.

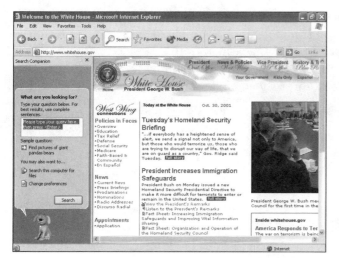

FIGURE 6-13

The Search Companion bar open in Internet Explorer.

Note To turn off the animated character, click the Change Preferences link, and then click the Without An Animated Screen Character link.

2 Click in the box, and then type a word, phrase, or sentence that describes what you want to search for. Click the Search button. Figure 6-14 shows the results I got when searching on "Internet statistics" with the Search Companion bar. As you can see, the Search Companion bar now presents a selection of more ways to broaden this search.

FIGURE 6-14

The Search Companion bar presents more options.

3 For purposes of this example, click the Automatically Send Your Search To Other Search Engines link. Figure 6-15 shows you still more options for broadening the search. You can click a link to send your search to AltaVista Search, HotBot, and FAST Search Engine. You can also click a link to send your search to still more search engines. (In the next section, I'll discuss some of these search engines.)

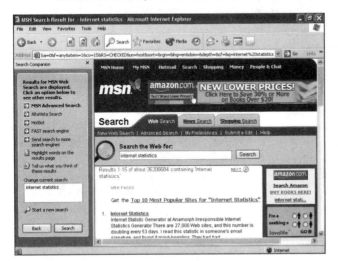

FIGURE 6-15

The Search Companion bar presents still more options.

At any point in your search, simply click the link to a page to open that resource. Notice in Figure 6-13 that you can also use the Search Companion to find items on your local computer.

Using an Internet Search Service

A search service is a term that describes a web site from which you can start a search of the Internet, and there are two types of search services:

- Search engines use programs to collect information about Web sites, and then an indexing program puts the information into a database. When you enter search criteria, the search engine looks in its database and displays a list of web pages that are relevant to your criteria.

- Directories are created by people rather than software alone. Individuals trained in cataloging determine how a web site and its contents should be classified, and place web sites in multilevel categories that you can browse.

You saw in Figure 6-15 that you could click a link to HotBot (http://hotbot.lycos.com) to send your search criteria to that service. HotBot is an example of a search engine. Yahoo! (http://www.yahoo.com) is an example of a directory search service, and an extremely popular search service, I might add.

Figure 6-16 shows the HotBot home page. As you can see, almost everything is at your fingertips on this page. You can search by keyword, you can use the HotBot directory, and you can restrict or expand your search using the options in the box on the left.

FIGURE 6-16

The HotBot home page.

Figure 6-17 shows the Yahoo! home page. Many Internet users have come to think of searching the Internet as synonymous with going to the Yahoo! site. At Yahoo! you can enter a search query in the box, or you can select from a hierarchy of categories and then search within a category.

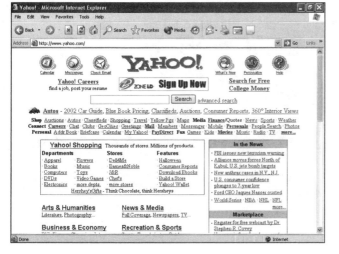

FIGURE 6-17

The Yahoo! home page.

AskJeeves (http://www.askjeeves.com) is the place to start if you think your search query has likely been asked before. At the home page, shown in Figure 6-18, simply type a question in the blank field and click Ask!

FIGURE 6-18

The AskJeeves home page.

Google is a goofy name for a search service, but what it does is not goofy. The Google search engine looks at all the web pages that link to a web site and then ranks those sites first when it returns search results. Google claims that an average search on this site takes only 0.04 seconds. Figure 6-19 shows the Google home page. To do a basic search, enter your keyword or phrase and press the Enter key.

FIGURE 6-19

The Google home page.

Customizing Internet Explorer

I mentioned earlier in this chapter that you customize Internet Explorer using the Internet Options dialog box, and I showed you how to use the Advanced tab in this dialog box to customize how a page is printed. In this section, I won't go into all the settings in the Internet Options dialog box, but I do want to show you some of the most useful settings.

As you saw earlier, Internet Explorer uses the MSN page as the start page by default. This may be one of the first things you want to change. For example, your broker might have a site that lets you track the progress (or lack thereof) of your securities, and you can set this page as your start page if that's the first thing you want to see when you start Internet Explorer. Or you might be on the lookout for cheap airline tickets. In this case, you could set as your start page a site that posts when routes you specify go below a certain price.

To change your start page, open the page that you want to become your start page, and then follow these steps:

1 In Internet Explorer, click the Tools menu, and then click Internet Options to open the Internet Options dialog box, which is shown in Figure 6-20.

FIGURE 6-20

The Internet Options dialog box, open at the General tab.

2 In the Home Page section, click the Use Current button, and then click OK.

If you don't have the new start page open but you know the URL of the page you want to use, you can instead enter the URL in the Address box. If at any time you want to return to using the MSN page, click the Use Default button. To use a blank start page, click the Use Blank button.

If you install another web browser in addition to Internet Explorer, it may configure itself as your default browser. In other words, you'll see it listed on the Start menu, and when you click an HTML file in an Explorer window, it will open in the newly installed browser. To specify which browser you want to use as your default browser, you use the options on the Programs tab in the Internet Options dialog box, which is shown in Figure 6-21. Click the arrow in one of the drop-down list boxes to select the program you want associated with a service.

FIGURE 6-21

The Internet Options dialog box, open at the Programs tab.

If you need to change any of your Internet connection settings, you can use the options on the Connections tab, which is shown in Figure 6-22. Clicking the Setup button starts the New Connection Wizard (discussed in Chapter 5).

FIGURE 6-22

The Internet Options dialog box, open at the Connections tab.

Chapter 7

Windows XP Accessories

Accessories are little programs you can use to create drawings, compose and edit documents, manage your computer, connect to the Internet or another computer, play audio CDs, play games, and more. In this chapter, we begin the discussion of Microsoft Windows XP accessories by talking about the following subjects:

- Finding the Windows accessory programs
- Using Calculator
- Editing simple text with Notepad
- Word processing with WordPad
- Creating and editing simple graphic images with Paint
- Faxing at the computer
- Running the Program Compatibility Wizard

Note   In Chapter 8, we'll take a close look at the accessories you can use to manage your computer (called System Tools), and then in Chapter 11 we'll explore music, multimedia, and what many people see as an essential life skill—how to play computer games.

7

Finding the Windows Accessory Programs

The Windows accessory programs appear on the Accessories submenu. To access Windows Accessories, follow these steps:

1 Click the Start button.

2 Point to All Programs.

3 Click Accessories.

Windows displays the submenu shown in Figure 7-1. To open an accessory, choose it from this submenu.

FIGURE 7-1

The Windows Accessories submenu.

Using Calculator

Windows Calculator is simply an on-screen version of the handheld item, and it works essentially in the same way. You can use it to perform standard and scientific or statistical operations.

Note   When you're working with Calculator, you can copy and paste calculations from it into other applications. From the Edit menu, choose Copy, and then in the other application, choose Paste from the Edit menu.

Starting Calculator

To open Calculator, choose it from the Accessories submenu. Figure 7-2 shows Calculator in Standard view. When you start Calculator, it opens in the view that was selected when it was last opened. For example, if you or somebody else was last using Calculator in Scientific view, that's how it opens when you start it again.

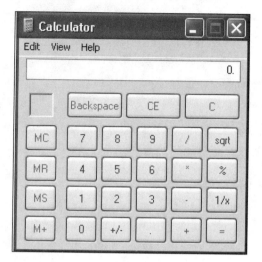

FIGURE 7-2

Calculator in Standard view.

Reviewing the Calculator Window

In both Standard and Scientific views, Calculator has the following keys:

- * represents the multiplication sign (x), and / represents the division sign (÷).
- Backspace deletes a single digit.
- CE deletes the last entry. You can also press the Delete key to delete the last entry.
- C removes a calculation all together. You can also press the Esc key to do this.
- MC clears a number from Calculator's memory.
- MR recalls a number from Calculator's memory.
- MS stores a number in Calculator's memory and removes whatever was already in memory.
- M+ adds a number to the number in Calculator's memory.

Note   You will probably find it easiest to use the mouse when working with Calculator, clicking the numbers and operators as you go along. But you can also use the keys across the top of the keyboard or on the numeric keypad. To use the keypad, Num Lock must be on. If it is not on, press the Num Lock key.

In Standard view, Calculator also has the following keys:

- sqrt calculates the square root of a number. For example, if you enter 36 and then click sqrt, the result is 6.
- % lets you add, subtract, divide, and multiply a number by a percentage. For example, if you enter 10+50% and click =, the result is 15.

- 1/x is the Inverse key. You use it to divide 1 by a value.

We'll look at Calculator in Scientific view in a later section. But now, let's put Calculator to work.

Computing with Calculator

Before we get started, to be sure that Calculator is in Standard view, click View and then click Standard if necessary. To add, subtract, multiply, divide, and perform any other standard arithmetic operations, follow these steps:

1 Enter the first number you want to use in the calculation.

2 Click the operator key (+, -, *, or /).

3 Enter the next number.

4 Click = to get the result.

If you want, you can store the result in memory. To do so, click MS. Calculator then displays M in the box above the memory keys, as shown in Figure 7-3. You can now use the other memory keys and the value in memory to continue calculating.

Note To clear Calculator's memory, click MC.

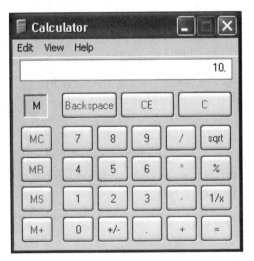

FIGURE 7-3

The value 10 is now stored in Calculator's memory.

Using Calculator in Scientific View

You use Calculator in Scientific view to calculate logarithms, convert values to other number systems, and to perform statistical calculations. When you choose the View menu's Scientific command, Windows opens Calculator in Scientific view, as shown in Figure 7-4.

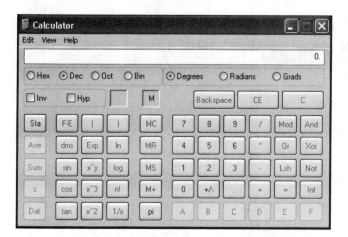

FIGURE 7-4

Calculator in Scientific view.

To perform a calculation, follow these steps:

1 Choose a number system from the option buttons in the upper left:
- Hex (hexadecimal)
- Dec (decimal)
- Oct (octal)
- Bin (binary)

2 Enter the first number, and then click an operator.

3 Continue to enter numbers and operators.

4 Click = to get the result.

To convert a value to another number system, for example, from decimal to hexadecimal, follow these steps:

1 Select a number system.

2 Enter the number you want to convert.

3 Click the option button that corresponds to the number system to which you want to convert.

Figure 7-5 shows the result of converting the decimal value 100 to hexadecimal.

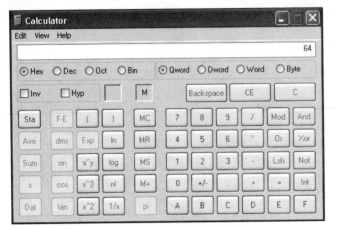

Note For information on how to use Calculator to perform statistical calculations, click the Help menu. To get help with any Calculator button, right-click it and then click What's This?

Using Notepad

Notepad is a simple text-editing program that you can use to create, view, and edit files. Notepad is handy for displaying the contents of the Clipboard, program files, ReadMe files, and your autoexec.bat and config.sys files. You can also use it when you want to quickly jot a note and print it.

In addition, you can use Notepad to handcode HTML. When you do so, there is no way that you can accidentally save special formatting, which is important when you are creating web pages. Special characters inserted in an HTML document may not appear when the page is opened in a web browser, and they can even produce errors. When you open a web page in Internet Explorer, click the View menu, and then click Source—the HTML document opens in Notepad.

Note Your autoexec.bat and config.sys files contain information that determines how your system is configured and boots up. If you aren't on speaking terms with these more technical concepts, it's best not to fiddle with these files.

To open Notepad, choose it from the Accessories submenu. Figure 7-6 shows a memo file open in the Notepad window.

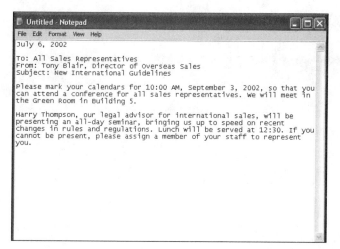

FIGURE 7-6

A memo file open in Notepad.

Editing Text with Notepad

To create a note in Notepad, just start typing. (When Notepad opens, the blinking cursor is at the beginning of the first line on your screen.) Press the Enter key to end a paragraph and start a new one. If you make a mistake while typing, press the Backspace key to delete the preceding character. To delete more—several characters, a sentence, or a paragraph—select the text by dragging the mouse over it and then press the Delete key.

You can do some formatting as you go along, or you can wait until you finish your note and then go back and add formatting. To add formatting to your note, follow these steps:

1 Select the text you want to format by dragging the mouse over it.

2 Choose the Format menu's Font command. Windows opens the Font dialog box, as shown in Figure 7-7.

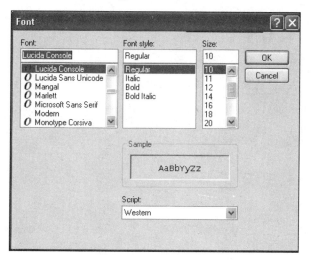

FIGURE 7-7

The Font dialog box.

3 In the Font dialog box, select a font, a font style, and a size, and click the OK button.

Note	To select your entire document so that you can apply formatting to it, choose the Edit menu's Select All command.

When you're finished with your note, you can save it (if you want) and print it. You save and print Notepad text files in the same way you save and print other documents.

Note	For more information about saving a file, refer to Chapter 3, "Files, Folders, and Disks." For more information about printing a document, refer to Chapter 4, "Printing."

Using Notepad's Other Commands

If you are working with a document that is more than a page or two, you can use Notepad's Page Setup command to add headers and footers and to insert the date and time in your document. To do so, follow these steps:

1 Choose the File menu's Page Setup command. Windows opens the Page Setup dialog box, as shown in Figure 7-8.

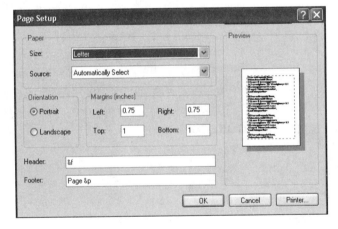

FIGURE 7-8

Enter header and footer information in the Page Setup dialog box.

2 In the Header and Footer boxes, type the letter and character combinations shown in Table 7-1 that correspond to the information you want.

To Do This	Type This
Insert the filename	&f
Insert the date	&d
Insert the time	&t
Insert page numbers	&p
Left-align the header or footer	&l
Center the header or footer	&c
Right-align the header or footer	&r

TABLE 7-1: Entering header and footer information.

3 Ensure that the paper size, orientation, and margins are to your liking, and click the OK button.

To simply insert the current time and date somewhere in your note, place the cursor in your note and choose the Edit menu's Time/Date command.

Notepad also includes a search feature. To locate specific text within a document, choose the Edit menu's Find command to open the Find dialog box. Enter the text you want to locate in the Find What box, and click the Find Next button. You can search up or down from the current position, and you can specify that Notepad match the case of the text just as you entered it in the Find What box.

Note If you open a file and portions of it scroll off the edge of the screen, choose the Format menu's Word Wrap command to keep all the text within view.

7

Using WordPad

WordPad is a word processor that comes with Windows. To start WordPad, choose it from the Accessories submenu. If you've used Microsoft Word (or any other Windows word processor, for that matter) the opening screen (see Figure 7-9 on the next page) will look familiar.

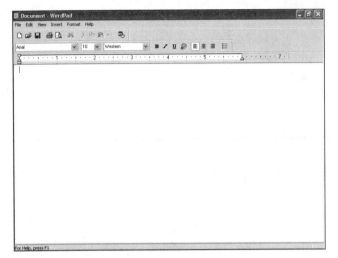

FIGURE 7-9

WordPad is a word processor that comes with Windows.

WordPad Basics

To create a document in WordPad, simply place your cursor in the document window and begin typing. That's all there is to it. You can issue commands to the WordPad program by using the Toolbar buttons, which are shown in Figure 7-10 and listed and described in Table 7-2, in order from left to right.

FIGURE 7-10

The Toolbar buttons.

Note Remember that you can point to a toolbar button to learn its name.

Button	What It Does
New	Opens a new, blank document.
Open	Opens an existing document.
Save	Saves your document.
Print	Prints your document.
Print Preview	Displays on-screen what your printed document will look like.
Find	Searches for text you specify.
Cut	Moves your selection to the Clipboard.
Copy	Duplicates your selection on the Clipboard.
Paste	Inserts the contents you've previously stored on the Clipboard at the insertion point.
Undo	Reverses your last action.
Date/Time	Inserts the current date and time.

TABLE 7-2: WordPad toolbar buttons.

The Format Bar shown in Figure 7-11 supplies tools you can use to add emphasis to your document.

FIGURE 7-11

The Format Bar.

As with Notepad, you can format as you go along, or you can enter the text of your document and then go back and format it. To format text, simply select the text by dragging the mouse over it and then choose one of the buttons on the Format Bar. Table 7-3, which follows, lists and describes each of the Format Bar drop-down lists and buttons in order from left to right. If you don't see the Format Bar on your screen, choose the View menu's Format Bar command.

Button	What It Does
Font	Displays a drop-down list of fonts you can use for the current text selection.
Font Size	Displays a drop-down list of font point sizes you can use for the current text selection.
Font Script	Displays a drop-down list of character sets you can use for the current text selection.
Bold	Boldfaces the current text selection.
Italic	Italicizes the current text selection.
Underline	Underlines the current text selection.
Color	Displays a list box of colors you can use to color the current text selection.
Align Left	Left-aligns the current text selection.
Center	Centers the current text selection.
Align Right	Right-aligns the current text selection.
Bullets	Turns the selected paragraphs into a list of bullet points.

TABLE 7-3: WordPad Format Bar buttons.

Word Processing with WordPad

Now that we've toured the WordPad window, let's create a document. We'll go through the steps to create the document shown in Figure 7-6, but you can, of course, use the same steps to create any document.

1   Choose the File menu's New command. Windows opens the New dialog box (see Figure 7-12).

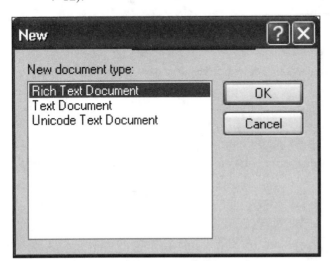

FIGURE 7-12

The New dialog box.

2   Make a selection from the three document types. For our purposes, select Text Document, and click the OK button.

3   Click the Date/Time button. Windows opens the Date And Time dialog box (see Figure 7-13).

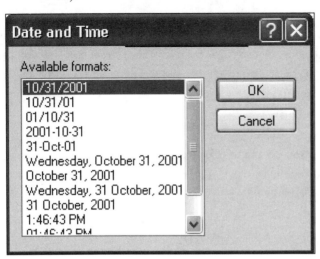

FIGURE 7-13

The Date And Time dialog box.

4 Select a format from the Available Formats list box, click the OK button, and then press the Enter key twice.

5 If you're re-creating the document in Figure 7-6, type the text in the To line, and press the Enter key; type the text in the From line, and press the Enter key; and type the text in the Subject line, and press the Enter key twice.

6 Type the body of the message, pressing the Enter key only to start a new paragraph. WordPad automatically wraps the text within a paragraph.

7 Choose the File menu's Save command to save your document.

Note Near the bottom of the File menu, WordPad maintains a list of the last four documents you've created. If you want to work on one of them, simply click the File menu and select the document from this list.

Note WordPad doesn't include a spelling checker, so be sure to proofread your documents before you distribute them.

Exploring WordPad's Formatting Tools

By default, WordPad uses the Times New Roman font in 10-point size. Let's increase this point size, choose a slightly more contemporary-looking font, and apply some other emphasis to this document. To do this, follow these steps:

1 Choose the Edit menu's Select All command.

2 Choose the Format menu's Font command. Windows opens the Font dialog box shown in Figure 7-14 (next page).

7

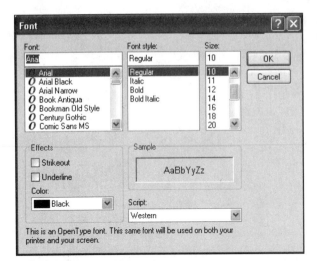

FIGURE 7-14

The Font dialog box.

3 In the Font list, click the up or down arrow to locate and select MS Sans Serif.

4 In the Size list, click 12, and then click the OK button.

5 Select the word *To,* and click the Bold toolbar button; select *From,* and click the Bold toolbar button; and then select *Subject,* and click the Bold toolbar button.

6 Select the time and date in the body of the memo, and click the Italic toolbar button.

7 Choose the File menu's Save command.

8 Click the Print toolbar button to print your document.

A memo is still a memo, but this one looks a bit more inviting now, don't you think?

Note   You can, of course, supply as much fancy formatting as you want to a document, but a judicious use of formatting is much more pleasing to the eye. Remember, too, that formatting should be appropriate to a document's content.

Note   Just like with Notepad, if you make a mistake while typing, press the Backspace key to delete the preceding character. To delete more—several characters, a sentence, or a paragraph— select the text by dragging the mouse over it and then press the Delete key.

Using WordPad's Other Commands

If you want to see what your document looks like before you print it, choose the File menu's Print Preview command. Figure 7-15 shows a document in Print Preview.

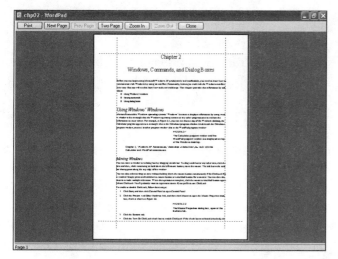

FIGURE 7-15

A document in Print Preview.

In this miniaturized version of the page, you can check the placement of your text, but you can't see the details. To get a better view, click the Zoom In button. If your document now pleases you, click the Print button to print it or click the Close button, which returns you to the normal view of your document.

If you want to change the margins, the paper size, the paper source, or the paper orientation, choose the File menu's Page Setup command to open the Page Setup dialog box (see Figure 7-16). After you make your changes, click the OK button to return to document view, or click the Printer button to specify a printer to use.

FIGURE 7-16

The Page Setup dialog box.

Note For more information on printing, see Chapter 4, "Printing."

Although creating a document and then printing it for distribution may be the most common use of a WordPad file, in Windows you can also send a WordPad document as e-mail or as an e-mail attachment. In these cases, or if you have a color printer, you might want to format a portion of your document in color. To do so, follow these steps:

1 Select the text you want to color.

2 Click the Color button on the Format Bar to open a drop-down list of color choices.

3 Click the color you want.

The selected text now appears in the color you selected.

WordPad's Edit menu contains a number of items that are common to most Windows applications:

- Undo
- Cut
- Copy
- Paste
- Paste Special
- Clear
- Select All

We've used some of their toolbar equivalents in this section. In addition, the Edit menu contains the Find, Find Next, and Replace commands—all of which come in handy if you want to make global changes to a document. For example, if you have a 20-page document that includes the abbreviation *ABC* and you want to change it to *ABC Association,* you can use Find and Replace to quickly do so without having to manually hunt for *ABC* and insert *Association.* To use Find and Replace, follow these steps:

1 Choose the Edit menu's Replace command. Windows opens the Replace dialog box (see Figure 7-17).

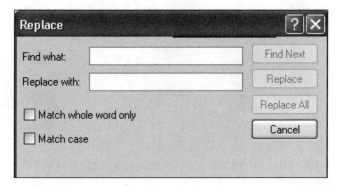

FIGURE 7-17
The Replace dialog box.

2 In the Find What box, type ABC.

3 In the Replace With box, type ABC Association.

4 Click the Replace All button.

When creating or editing a document in WordPad, you can insert any of a number of objects, including the following:

- A bitmap image
- Another WordPad document
- Clip art
- A Microsoft Word document
- A video clip
- A wave sound

To insert an object, choose the Insert menu's Object command to open the Insert Object dialog box (see Figure 7-18).

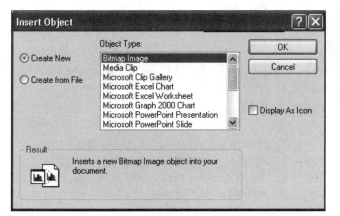

FIGURE 7-18
The Insert Object dialog box.

Click the Create New option button to select the type of object and activate the program for creating it. For example, selecting Bitmap Image from the list box opens the Paint program.

Click the Create From File option button to insert an object from an existing file. If you select the Display As Icon check box, WordPad inserts an icon in the document rather than the actual content. Click the icon to open the object.

Let's take a break from numbers and words and look at a Windows accessory that lets you exercise some creativity in the visual arts.

Using Paint

Paint is a program you can use to develop and edit graphic images—simple diagrams, logos, scanned photographs, even complex artistic creations. You're limited only by your imagination (and, well, maybe a bit by your native talents). You can create something from scratch, or you can modify existing images. You can even use a Paint creation as your desktop wallpaper.

Getting Started with Paint

To start Paint, choose it from the Accessories submenu. You'll see the Paint window, as shown in Figure 7-19 on the next page, with a blank canvas ready for your artistic endeavors.

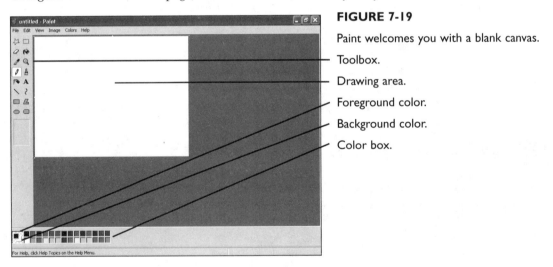

FIGURE 7-19

Paint welcomes you with a blank canvas.

Toolbox.

Drawing area.

Foreground color.

Background color.

Color box.

When you work with an image in Paint, the tools of your trade are, quite logically, in the toolbox (see Figure 7-20). Each is the electronic equivalent of the tool you might use if you were working in the physical realm of paper or canvas. Table 7-4 lists and describes each of the Paint toolbox tools. (Remember that you can point to a tool to learn its name.)

FIGURE 7-20

The Toolbox.

Tool	What It Does
Free-Form Select	Selects an irregularly shaped area of the image.
Select	Selects a rectangular-shaped area of the image.
Eraser/Color Eraser	Removes an area of the image as you move the eraser over it.
Fill With Color	Fills an area with the color you selected.
Pick Color	Selects the color of an object you click.
Magnifier	Enlarges the area you select.
Pencil	Draws a freehand line one pixel wide.
Brush	Draws lines of different shapes and widths.
Airbrush	Draws using an airbrush of the size you select.
Text	Inserts text into an image.
Line	Draws a straight line. (Hold down the Shift key to create a really straight line.)
Curve	Draws a curved line.
Rectangle	Draws a rectangle. (Choose Rectangle, and hold down the Shift key to draw a square.)
Polygon	Draws a figure of straight lines connecting at any angle.
Ellipse	Draws an ellipse (Choose Ellipse, and hold down the Shift key to draw a circle.)
Rounded Rectangle	Draws a rectangle that has curved corners.

TABLE 7-4: Paint toolbox tools.

7

If you're like most of us, however, you won't find your favorite drawing tool in the toolbox. It's in the Edit menu, and it's the Undo command. The keyboard shortcut for Undo is Ctrl+Z.

Note   If you are totally dissatisfied with what you are doing, choose the Edit menu's Select All command and press the Delete key to erase all your squiggles from the canvas.

Creating a Simple Image

Okay, let's try it. To create a graphic image with Paint, follow these general steps:

1 Choose the File menu's New command.

2 Optionally, choose the Image menu's Attributes command. Windows opens the Attributes dialog box (see Figure 7-21) in which you establish the size and shape of your picture. Click the OK button after you set the size and shape.

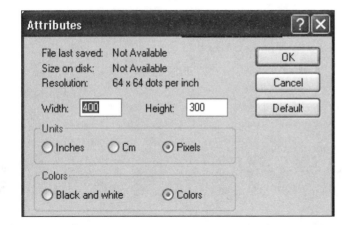

FIGURE 7-21

The Attributes dialog box.

3 Click a drawing tool to select it.

4 Choose a line width, brush shape, or rectangle type from the toolbox.

5 Choose a foreground color by clicking a color in the color box.

6 Choose a background color by right-clicking a color in the color box.

7 Start drawing.

8 When you're finished, choose the File menu's Save As command. Windows opens the Save As dialog box.

9 Select a format in which to save your drawing. By default, Paint proposes to save the image using the maximum number of colors that your system can display.

10 Click the Save button.

Figure 7-22 shows a simple image created in Paint:

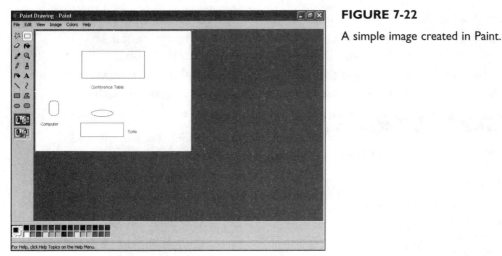

FIGURE 7-22

A simple image created in Paint.

Note To change the font or point size, before typing the text, choose the View menu's Text Toolbar command. Then choose a font and font size.

Although the steps are straightforward, you'll find it takes a little practice to place objects exactly where you want them. When you make a mistake, rub it out with the Eraser tool, or choose the Edit menu's Undo command. Or choose the Edit menu's Select All command, and press the Delete key.

Faxing at the Computer

To send and receive faxes from your computer, all you need is a fax modem. If you bought your computer within the last couple of years, your modem is probably also a fax modem. To verify that your modem can be used to send and receive faxes, open the Printers and Faxes folder (click the Start button, click Control Panel, and then click Printers and Faxes). If you see a Fax icon, your modem is a fax modem.

If you upgraded from an earlier version of Windows that already included fax, the operating system automatically detected your fax modem, installed the fax service, and installed the associated printer. If you made a new installation of Windows, you may have to install the fax components of Windows separately. In the Printer Tasks bar, click the Set Up Faxing link to open the Configuring Components screen. Setup will begin configuring the Fax Services. When the configuration is complete, you'll see a Fax icon in your Printers and Faxes folder.

Configuring Fax

The first time you use the fax service, you need to do some setup. Follow these steps:

1 In the Printers And Faxes folder, click the Send A Fax link in the Printer Tasks bar to start the Fax Configuration Wizard. At the Welcome screen, click Next.

2 Enter the information you want to use on your fax cover page, including your name, address, fax number, e-mail address and so on, as shown in Figure 7-23. Click Next.

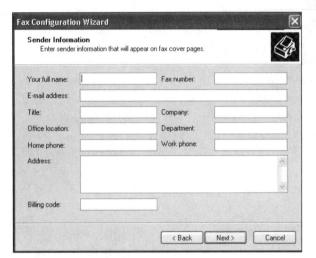

FIGURE 7-23

Enter user information into the Sender Information screen.

3 Click the drop-down arrow to select the modem you want to use. Most people only have one modem installed in their computer so this is usually an easy choice. Click the Enable Send and Enable Receive check boxes as appropriate. If you choose to receive faxes, specify how many rings you want the fax modem to wait before answering. Two rings is a pretty typical setting, but it depends on how you use the telephone line and whether the line is shared with other devices or a handset for voice calls. Click Next.

4 Enter either your fax number or your company name into the TSID field. This information will be sent along with your fax and will be printed at the top of each page as your fax is printed out at the receiving location. Click Next.

5 If you selected to receive faxes, enter either your fax number or your company name into the CSID field. This information will be sent to the sending fax machine. Click Next.

6 When you receive a fax, you can send it to a printer or you can store a copy of the fax in a folder to work on later. Specify your options, and then click Next.

7 The wizard displays a summary of all the information you have entered. If the information is correct, click Finish to close the wizard, otherwise click Back and correct the information.

Sending a Fax

You can fax a document from any Windows application that includes a Print menu. Here are the steps to follow to send a fax from Notepad:

1 Create a document or open an existing document to fax.

2 Click the File menu, and then click Print to open the Print dialog box. Select the Fax icon and choose Print to open the Send Fax Wizard. Click Next.

3 Fill in the To, Fax Number, and dialing information, as shown in Figure 7-24, and click Next. If you are sending the same fax to several recipients, enter information for each of the recipients and then click Add. You can also select a recipient from the list and click Remove to remove them from this list. Click Next.

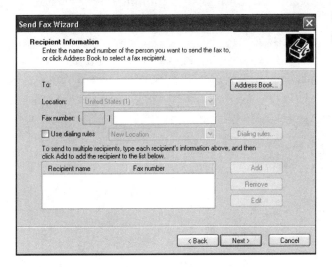

FIGURE 7-24

Enter recipient and dialing information.

4 In the Preparing the Cover Page screen of the wizard, specify whether you want to include a cover page and, if so, what it should contain. Use the Cover Page Template drop-down list box to select a type of cover page. Add text for the subject line. When you're finished, click Next.

5 In the Schedule screen, specify when you want to send the fax and its priority. Click Next.

6 The wizard displays a summary of all the information you have entered. If the information is correct, click Finish to close the wizard, otherwise click Back and correct the information. You can also click Preview to see an on-screen image of your fax. This is a very convenient way to check that you will be sending exactly what you thought you would be sending.

Note You can track the progress of the fax using the Fax Monitor dialog box, which appears on your screen as the fax is dispatched.

Using the Program Compatibility Wizard

If you have used previous versions of Windows and are like most of us, you have favorite programs that were developed for and run under these previous versions. In most cases, these programs will run just fine when you install them on a Windows XP system. For those cases when they don't run just fine, you can run them in Compatibility Mode. Compatibility Mode is a feature that sort of "tricks" the program into thinking it is running on the version of Windows for which it was created.

To run a program in Compatibility Mode, follow these steps:

1 Click Start, click All Programs, click Accessories, and then click Program Compatibility Wizard to open the wizard in Help and Support Center at the Welcome screen. Click Next to open the next screen of the wizard, which is shown in Figure 7-25.

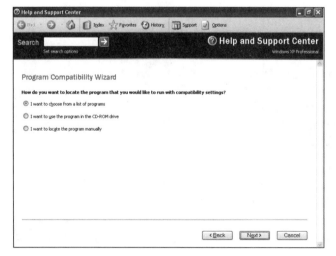

FIGURE 7-25

Tell the wizard how to locate the program.

2 Click an option button to tell the wizard how to locate the program, and then click Next to open the next screen of the wizard, which is shown in Figure 7-26.

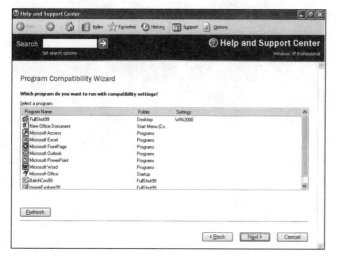

FIGURE 7-26

Select the program.

3 Select the program, and then click Next to open the next screen of the wizard, which is shown in Figure 7-27.

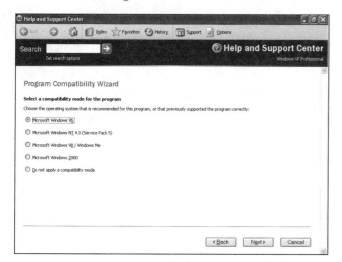

FIGURE 7-27

Select the operating system.

4 Choose the operating system under which your application originally ran, and then click Next.

5 If the program you want to run is a game or an educational program, you can select the display settings in the next screen. Otherwise, just click Next.

6 In the next screen, you will see the complete path to your application and the name of the Windows operating system you will be using for the compatibility test. Click Next to start your program running in this mode. Once you have determined that the application works as expected in this mode, close your application and click Next.

7 If your application worked as expected, you can make Windows start the application in Compatibility Mode automatically every time you start the program. Click Yes to update the shortcut so that Compatibility Mode is used automatically, or click No so that Compatibility Mode is not used. Click Finish, and you are done.

Chapter 8

System Tools

The Microsoft Windows XP system tools help you to maintain your computer and the Windows operating system. In this way, you keep your computer and the Windows operating system running smoothly and dependably. Although Windows lets you do lots of different types of maintenance, I'll limit my discussion to the most common and important maintenance tasks:

- Protecting your computer from viruses
- Defragmenting your disk
- Clearing your disk of unnecessary files
- Scheduling Windows maintenance
- Monitoring your computer usage
- Viewing your System Information
- Using Windows Update
- Restoring your system
- Backing up and restoring

Protecting Your Computer from Viruses

A virus is a malevolent program that can attach itself to your computer system without your knowledge or permission and wipe out all of your work in less than a minute. Computer viruses are not airborne; they travel via infected disk, e-mail, files you download from the Internet, and, in rare instances, even in shrink-wrapped software. Many recent viruses replicate themselves by reading a recipient's address book and mailing themselves to all the people in it.

In addition to faithfully adhering to your back up schedule, which I'll describe at the end of this chapter, what can you do to avoid falling prey to computer viruses? Here are some ideas:

- Acquire, install, and use antivirus software regularly. And keep it up-to-date by regularly downloading any new virus definitions provided by the maker of your antivirus software. New viruses are being created and discovered all the time, and your software needs to know about them.
- Protect the integrity of your home computer or office and your office computer or net-

work. It is common to catch a workplace virus and bring it home or to acquire a virus at home and then infect the office network. For just this reason, many computers on corporate networks don't even have floppy drives.

- Never download a file or a program if you don't know and trust the source.
- If an application supports it, turn on Macro Virus Protection.
- Don't believe everything you hear. There are as many hoaxes about viruses as there are viruses. To stay current, go to on of the antivirus software vendor's sites or check the Symantec AntiVirus Research Center's Web site at www.symantec.com/avcenter/.

Defragmenting Your Disk

When you save a file to your disk, all of the file's information doesn't always end up in the same place. Often the file gets broken into fragments and saved in pieces. The problem with this is that the longer you use your computer and the more you create and delete files, the more scattered your files become on your hard disk. Every time you want to open a file, your computer has to pull up all the bits and pieces of the file from different places on your disk. This fragmentation slows down your computer.

To solve the problem of fragmentation, you use the Disk Defragmenter. The Disk Defragmenter looks through the files on your disk and puts matching pieces together. This frees up larger chunks of space and makes files open more quickly. To use the Disk Defragmenter, follow these steps:

1 Click the Start button.

2 Point to All Programs, and point to Accessories.

3 Point to System Tools, and click Disk Defragmenter to open Disk Defragmenter, as shown in Figure 8-1.

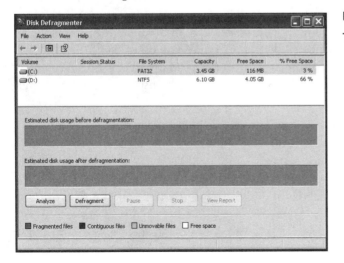

FIGURE 8-1

The Disk Defragmenter program.

4 Select the drive you want to defragment, and then click the Analyze button. Disk Defragmenter takes a look at the selected disk and then reports on its findings in a message box, as shown in Figure 8-2.

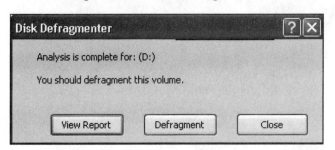

FIGURE 8-2

Disk Defragmenter reports that the disk should be defragmented.

5 To see details before you defragment, click the View Report button. Windows displays the Analysis Report dialog box, a sample of which is shown in Figure 8-3.

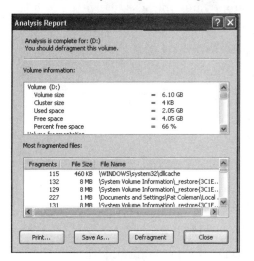

FIGURE 8-3

Windows reports its findings in the Analysis Report dialog box.

6 Close the Analysis Report dialog box, and then click Defragment to begin the process. The bar at the bottom of the screen shows the progress.

If you have a large or badly fragmented drive, the defragment can take some time. It's best to run Disk Defragmenter when you've finished work for the day or when you otherwise don't need to be using your computer. You can do other work during the process, although your response will be slower. Also, whenever you save a file, Disk Defragmenter will start all over again. How often should you run Disk Defragmenter? Any time it seems that your system is slowing down or otherwise experiencing problems. Under normal circumstances, once a month should be sufficient.

Clearing Your Disk of Unnecessary Files

You can also free up space on your hard disk by deleting unnecessary files. The Disk Cleanup tool helps you do this by searching through the folders that tend to hold files you can safely remove. It then tells you how much space you can create by deleting these files.

To use the Disk Cleanup tool, follow these steps:

1 Click the Start button.

2 Point to All Programs, and point to Accessories.

3 Point to System Tools, and then click Disk Cleanup to open the Select Drive dialog box, as shown in Figure 8-4.

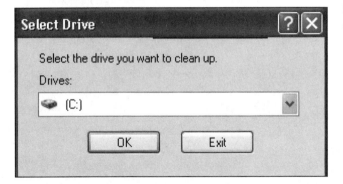

FIGURE 8-4

The Select Drive dialog box.

4 Select the hard disk you want to clean up from the Drives drop-down list box and click the OK button. The Disk Cleanup tool scans your disk for files you can probably get rid of and displays a dialog box telling you what you can delete and how much space you will gain, as shown in Figure 8-5.

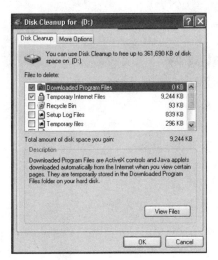

FIGURE 8-5

Disk Cleanup reports.

5 Select the check boxes next to the folders containing the files you want to delete.

Note   To check out which files you're deleting before you delete them (a good idea), click the View Files button.

---

6 Click the More Options tab if you want to uninstall Windows accessories and other programs you no longer use.

7 Click the OK button to delete the contents of the folders you selected.

Scheduling Windows Maintenance

You can schedule Windows maintenance so that tools such as antivirus programs run automatically on a regular basis. To do this, you use the Scheduled Task tool to tell Windows which programs you want it to run automatically and when you want it to run them.

Adding a Scheduled Task

You can add any program on your computer to your list of scheduled tasks so that it runs according to the schedule you specify. For instance, you might want to add a file management program or an antivirus program. To schedule a task, follow these steps:

1 Click the Start button.

2 Point to All Programs, and point to Accessories.

3 Point to System Tools, and then click Scheduled Tasks to open the Scheduled Tasks folder, as shown in Figure 8-6.

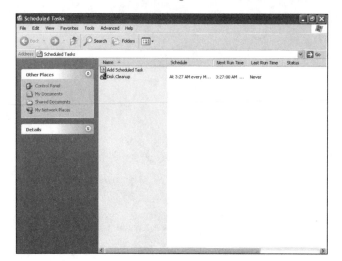

FIGURE 8-6

The Scheduled Tasks folder.

4 Double-click Add Scheduled Task to start the Scheduled Task Wizard, as shown in Figure 8-7.

FIGURE 8-7

The Schedule Task Wizard.

5 Click the Next button to open the screen shown in Figure 8-8.

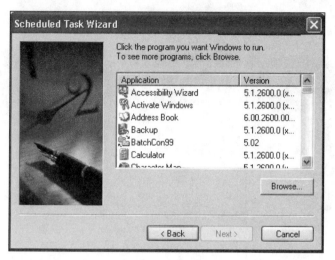

FIGURE 8-8

Select the task you want to schedule.

6 Select the program you want to schedule from the list, and click the Next button to open the screen shown in Figure 8-9.

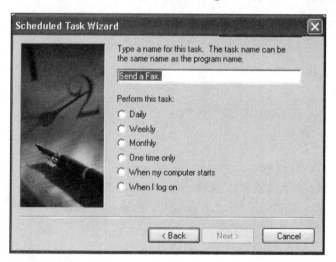

FIGURE 8-9

The Scheduled Tasks Wizard lets you name and create a schedule for the task.

8

7 Enter a name for the task, specify when you want the task to occur, and click the Next button to open the screen shown in Figure 8-10.

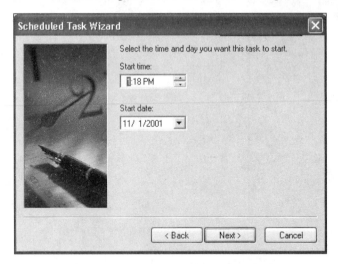

FIGURE 8-10

Select the day and time.

8 Specify the day and time you want the task to occur, and click the Next button.

9 Click the Finish button.

Using Scheduled Tasks

You can change the scheduling properties for any program you've added to your list of Scheduled Tasks. To do so, follow these steps:

1 Click the Start button.

2 Point to All Programs, and point to Accessories.

3 Point to System Tools, and click Scheduled Tasks to open the Scheduled Tasks folder.

4 Double-click a task in the list to open its dialog box. Figure 8-11 shows the dialog box that opens when you have scheduled Disk Cleanup.

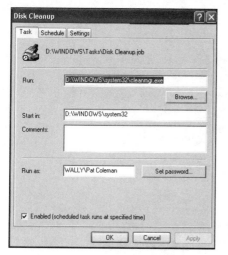

FIGURE 8-11

The Disk Cleanup dialog box.

5 Click the Schedule tab (see Figure 8-12).

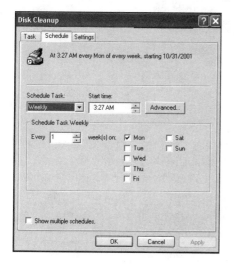

FIGURE 8-12

The Disk Cleanup dialog box, open at the Schedule tab.

6 Use the Schedule Task drop-down list box to specify whether you want the task to occur daily, weekly, or monthly. Or you can use this drop-down list box to specify a different occurrence schedule. For example, you can specify that you want the task to occur every time you log on to Windows or every time your computer is idle.

7 Enter the time of day you want the task to occur in the Start Time box.

8 Use the boxes in the Schedule Task section to specify the day or date on which you want the task to occur.

9 Click the Settings tab (see Figure 8-13).

FIGURE 8-13

The Disk Cleanup dialog box, open at the Settings tab.

10 Specify what to do with the task on the list after you complete it.

11 Specify whether you want the task to occur only when you are not using your computer.

12 Specify whether you want the task to occur while your computer is running on batteries.

13 Click the OK button.

Monitoring Your Computer Usage

Windows XP comes with a tool you can use to monitor the usage of programs and resources on your computer: Task Manager. To open Task Manager, press Ctrl+Alt+Delete. If you have a previous version of Windows other than Windows 2000 Professional, you're probably thinking, "Hey, I don't want to reboot my computer!" Well, this key sequence works differently in Windows XP—it opens Task Manager. You can also open Task Manager in the following ways:

- Right-click the Taskbar, and choose Task Manager from the shortcut menu.
- Click the Start button, click Run, in the Open box, type *tskmgr*, and click OK.

Figure 8-14 shows Task Manager open at the Applications tab. (If more than one user is currently logged on to your computer, you will also see a Users tab.)

FIGURE 8-14

Task Manager, open at the Applications tab.

You will probably most often use the Applications tab to close an application that has stopped running properly. In the Status column of the Applications tab, each open application is identified as Running or Not Responding. To close an open application that is misbehaving, select it, and then click the End Task button.

You can also use Task Manager to monitor all the running processes on your computer, including application processes and processes that Windows XP runs automatically. To do so, click the Processes tab, which is shown in Figure 8-15.

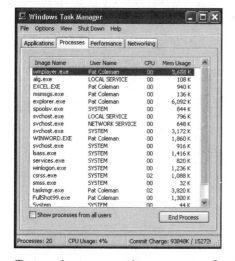

FIGURE 8-15

Task Manager, open at the Processes tab.

To terminate a running process, select it, and then click the End Process button.

Note	Don't end a process unless you really know what you are doing. Terminating a running process can crash other programs that are running correctly if they depend on that process.

To get a really good picture of your computer's usage, click the Performance tab (see Figure 8-16). This tab graphically shows how your computer is using memory, processor time, and other resources.

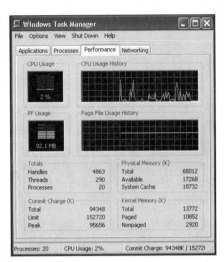

FIGURE 8-16

Task Manager, open at the Performance tab.

The Networking tab in Task Manager (see Figure 8-17) monitors Internet usage (if the computer has an Internet connection) and local area network usage (if the computer is part of a local area network). At the bottom of the tab Task Manager reports the link speed and the number of bytes transferred for each network adapter.

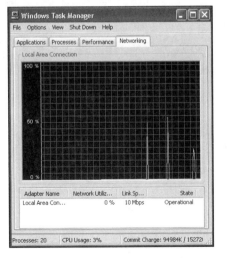

FIGURE 8-17

Task Manager, open at the Networking tab.

When you have multiple windows open on the desktop and then open Task Manager, Task Manager opens on top of all the other windows, by default. If you prefer for Task Manager not to open on top, click the Options menu, and then click Always On Top to clear the check mark.

Sometimes it's also handy to use the Shut Down menu in Task Manager. The Shut Down menu has the following commands:

- Hibernate
- Turn Off
- Restart
- Log Off *User*
- Lock Computer

Note Locking the computer in Windows XP leaves the current session running and quickly displays the Welcome screen. You can also lock the computer by pressing Winkey+L.

Viewing Your System Information

System Information provides you with a quick and easy run-down of what you have installed on your computer and to what extent you're using your computer's resources. If you ever need to give a technical support person the correct details about how your computer is set up and working, System Information is a good place to turn.

To use System Information, follow these steps:

1 Click the Start button.

2 Point to All Programs, and point to Accessories.

3 Point to System Tools, and click System Information. The System Information window (see Figure 8-18, next page) displays details about the version of Windows you're using, the name of your computer, the user name you used to log on, what kind of processor you have, how much memory is installed on your computer, the percentage of your resources that is free, and so on.

8

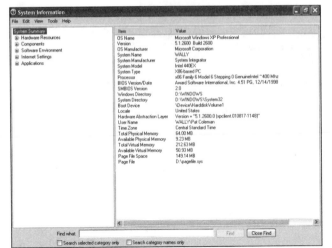

FIGURE 8-18

The System Information window.

4 Click a plus sign (+) to view the categories within a subject.

5 Select a topic to read its information.

6 To print what System Information displays, click the File menu, and then click Print.

Using Windows Update

Windows Update is a feature that, by default, automatically downloads and installs updates to Windows when an Administrator is logged on. These updates may include patches, fixes for security problems, and the like. You can also run Windows Update manually, and I'll show you how to set that up shortly. Regardless of whether Windows Update runs automatically or manually, though, here's how it works:

- Windows Update goes to the Microsoft site to check which updates are available.
- The available updates are compared with what is currently on your system.
- If your computer needs these updates, Windows Update downloads them to your computer.
- Windows Update notifies you that the updates have been downloaded and asks you to install them.

To tell Windows XP how and when you want Windows Update to run, follow these steps:

I Click the Start button, right-click My Computer, and then choose Properties from the shortcut menu to open the System Properties dialog box, which is shown in Figure 8-19.

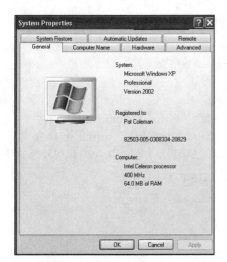

FIGURE 8-19

The System Properties dialog box, open at the General tab.

2 Click the Automatic Updates tab, which is shown in Figure 8-20.

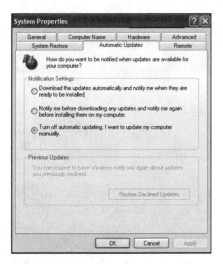

FIGURE 8-20

The System Properties dialog box, open at the Automatic Updates tab.

3 In the Notification Settings section, you have the following options:

- Download The Updates Automatically And Notify Me When They Are Ready To Be Installed. This option is selected by default, and you might want to leave it selected if you want to use automatic updating and have a fast Internet connection.

- Notify Me Before Downloading Any Updates And Notify Me Again Before Installing Them On My Computer. If you don't have a fast connection or just don't like things happening to your computer without your knowledge, you might want to select this option.

- Turn Off Automatic Updating. I Want To Update My Computer Manually. Select this option if you don't want to use Windows Update at all or if you want to choose when to run it.

4 If you have previously declined updates, you can click the Restore Declined Updates button to make these updates available again.

5 Click OK.

To run Windows Update manually, click the Start button, click All Programs, and then click Windows Update. You'll then see the Windows Update page, which will look similar to that in Figure 8-21. Follow the on-screen instructions to check for, download, and install updates.

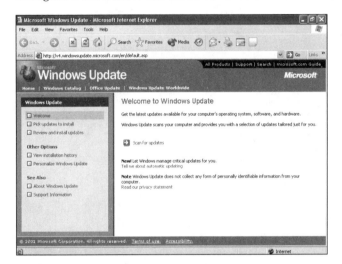

FIGURE 8-21

The Windows Update page.

Restoring Your System

System Restore is a Windows XP feature that first appeared in Windows Me. If you suddenly have trouble getting into Windows, you can use System Restore to return to the settings that were in place when Windows was last working properly. In my office I have Windows Me running on one of my computers, and I'm sorry to report that I've had to resort to System Restore many, many times on that computer. In contrast, I've been running Windows XP for months and months now on another computer in my office, and I've never had to run System Restore. As you may have heard, Windows XP is supposed to be the most stable and reliable Windows operating system ever, and thus far in my experience, that seems to be the case. Nevertheless, no operating system is perfect, and when the inevitable occurs, you want to be prepared by knowing what to do; that is, by knowing how to run System Restore.

Note System Restore restores only system files, not data files. Be sure that you back up your data files regularly to another medium such as a CD, a floppy disk, another drive on your network, a zip drive, or tape.

Although you can run System Restore manually even when your system is working properly, it's best not to do so. It's best to run System Restore only when something goes seriously wrong. In such a case, follow these steps:

1 When you see a message on a black screen that says "For troubleshooting and advanced startup options for Windows XP Professional, press F8," press F8.

2 You'll see a menu that includes the option to boot into Safe Mode. Select that option.

Note Safe Mode loads only a minimal number of items that are necessary to boot the computer.

3 As Safe Mode loads, you'll have the choice of working in Safe Mode or using System Restore. Click No to use System Restore and to open System Restore at the Welcome screen, as shown in Figure 8-22.

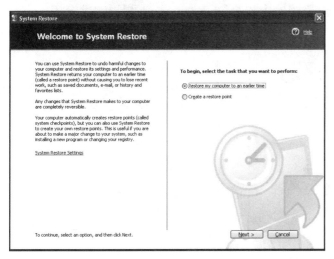

FIGURE 8-22

Starting System Restore.

8

4 Click Next to open the Select A Restore Point screen, as shown in Figure 8-23.

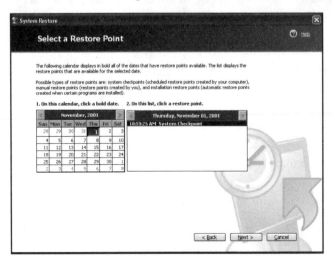

FIGURE 8-23

Selecting a restore point.

5 If no restore points have been created for the current day, click a boldface date on the calendar, and then, from the list on the right, select a time. Click Next to open the Confirm Restore Point Selection screen, as shown in Figure 8-24.

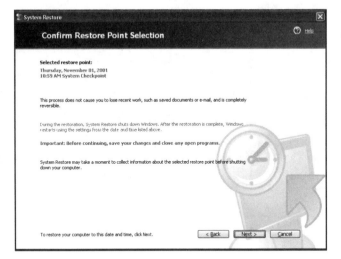

FIGURE 8-24

Confirming your restore point.

6 If you are ready to restore, click Next.

Note During the restoration process, don't do anything else at your computer.

7 When the restoration is complete, you'll see a message to that effect, and Windows XP will restart.

Setting Restore Points

You can also set your own restore points. You might consider doing so if you are about to make some major change to your system so that if all does not go well, you can return to the settings that were in place before you made the changes. To set a restore point, follow these steps:

1 Click the Start button, click All Programs, click Accessories, click System Tools, and then click System Restore to open the Welcome To System Restore screen, as shown earlier in Figure 8-22.

2 Click the Create A Restore Point option, and then click Next to open the Create A Restore Point screen, as shown in Figure 8-25.

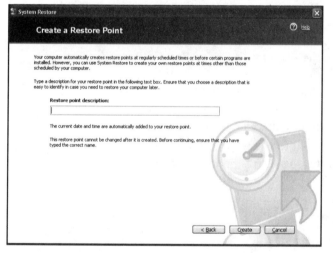

FIGURE 8-25

Enter a description of the restore point.

3 In the Restore Point Description box, enter a descriptive title for your restore point, and then click Create. Windows creates the restore point and adds the current date and time to the description.

Changing Settings for System Restore

Windows XP enables System Restore by default and sets a certain amount of disk space for saving restore points. You can change either setting if you want, although I suggest that you always keep System Restore enabled. To modify the settings, follow these steps:

1 Click the Start button, right-click My Computer, and then choose Properties from the shortcut menu to open the System Properties dialog box.

2 Click the System Restore tab, as shown in Figure 8-26.

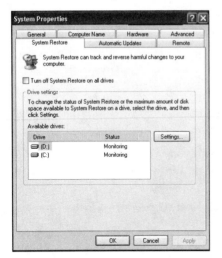

FIGURE 8-26

The System Properties dialog box, open at the System Restore tab.

Note   You can also open the System Properties dialog box at the System Restore tab by clicking the System Restore Settings link in the Welcome To System Restore screen.

---

3 To disable System Restore, click the Turn Off System Restore On All Drives check box. (If you have multiple drives on a computer, System Restore must be enabled or disabled on all drives. You can't turn it off for one drive and on for another.)

4 To change the amount of space allotted to a drive for System Restore, select the drive and then click the Settings button to open Drive Settings dialog box, as shown in Figure 8-27.

FIGURE 8-27

Changing the disk space allotted to System Restore.

5 Move the slider to reflect the amount of space you want allotted, and then click OK.

6 Click OK again in the System Properties dialog box.

Backing Up and Restoring Files

In you work in a large enterprise, in all likelihood your employer has a plan in place for backing up and restoring all data and system information that is part of a larger disaster recovery policy. Files are backed up on a regular schedule and often stored off site in a safe place. This process is usually a task assigned to a backup operator who is totally responsible for it, and you don't need to keep other backups. But if you are using your computer in a home office, a small office, or even just for you own personal enjoyment, you'll want to take measures to ensure that important information is not lost in the event of a disaster. Obviously, fire, flood, or an earthquake qualifies as a disaster, but you can also lose information by accidental deletion, overwriting a file with a previous version, or a hard-disk crash. Also, as I mentioned at the beginning of this chapter, a virus can wipe out your hard drive in less than a minute.

As I mentioned in Chapter 3, it's a good idea to back up your data files regularly to a CD, if you have a CD drive. You can also store files at certain sites on the Internet. In addition, Windows XP comes with a wizard that you can use to easily backup and restore individual files, your documents and settings, the documents and settings of all the people who use the computer, and all information on the computer. A floppy disk is not the medium of choice for most of these kinds of backups, but if you have a writable CD drive or other medium that can hold a lot of data, you're in business.

To use the wizard to back up, follow these steps:

1 Click the Start button, click All Programs, click Accessories, click System Tools, and then click Backup to start the Backup Or Restore Wizard, as shown in Figure 8-28.

FIGURE 8-28

Starting the wizard.

8

2 At the Welcome screen click Next to open the Backup Or Restore screen, as shown in Figure 8-29.

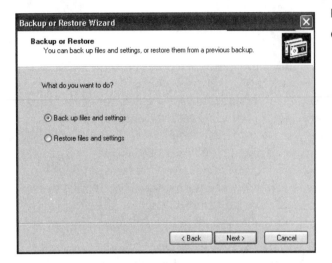

FIGURE 8-29

Choosing to back up files and settings.

3 Click the Back Up Files And Settings option, and then click Next to open the What To Back Up screen, as shown in Figure 8-30.

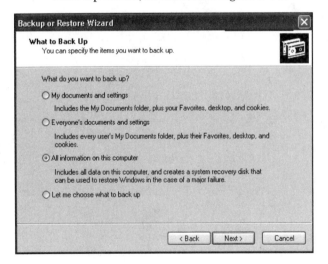

FIGURE 8-30

Choose what to back up.

4 Click the option button that corresponds with what you want to back up. For purposes of this example, I'll back up all the information on the computer. Click Next to open the Backup Type, Destination, And Name screen, as shown in Figure 8-31.

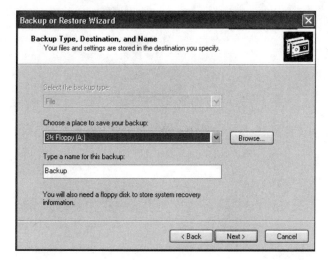

FIGURE 8-31

Choosing a backup medium and type.

5 If you have not made a backup of this information previously, the first option will be unavailable. If you have made a previous backup of this information, you can click the drop-down arrow to choose the backup type from a list.

6 Select the medium to which you'll back up from the Choose A Place To Save Your Backup drop-down list, and then enter a name for the backup. Click Next to open the Completing The Backup Or Restore Wizard screen.

7 Click Finish to begin the backup.

When the backup is complete, remove the medium and store it in a safe place, preferably away from your computer and in a location that you aren't like to forget.

Restoring from a Backup

To restore a file that you have backed up, start the Backup Or Restore Wizard as described in the previous section, and click Next. On the Backup Or Restore screen, click the Restore Files And Settings option. Click Next and then follow the wizard's instructions.

Chapter 9

Troubleshooting Windows XP

When you're stumped trying to figure out how to do something in Windows XP, the first place to look for answers is Help and Support Center. If you've used previous versions of Windows, you'll find that Help is vastly improved and enhanced. It now includes features that let you search the Microsoft Knowledge Base, access remote assistance from a friend or colleague, and step through a number of troubleshooters to take care tasks as common as printing and as complicated as setting up a local area network. In addition, Help and Support Center works like a web page, giving you quick and easy access to the information you need on a particular topic.

This chapter describes how to get help in the following ways:

- Using Help and Support Center
- Getting Support
- Using the troubleshooters
- Getting help on the Internet

Using Help and Support Center

To open Help and Support Center, click the Start button, and then click Help and Support. Figure 9-1 shows the home page of Help and Support Center.

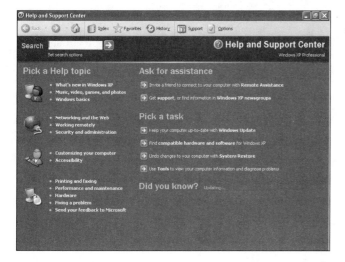

FIGURE 9-1

The home page of Help and Support Center.

The buttons on the Standard toolbar will look familiar if you've used Internet Explorer. In order from left to right, you use them to do the following:

- Clicking the Back and Forward buttons display the previous or next page you were viewing.
- Clicking the Home button displays the home page shown in Figure 9-1.
- Clicking Index opens the page shown in Figure 9-2. Enter a search term in the Type In The Keyword To Find box, and the list moves to the alphabetic area that contains the keyword. Double-click a topic to display its contents in the pane on the right.

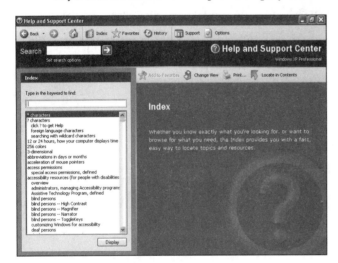

FIGURE 9-2

Searching the index.

- Clicking Favorites opens the Favorites bar in a pane on the left of the window, which displays any help topics you've added to this list. The Favorites list is a handy device with which you can quickly access a topic rather than searching for it again. Once a topic is in the Favorites list, all you need to do to open it is to click it. I'll show you how to add a topic to the Favorites list later in this chapter.
- Clicking History displays the History bar, which shows a list of the items you most recently opened. Figure 9-3 shows a sample History bar.

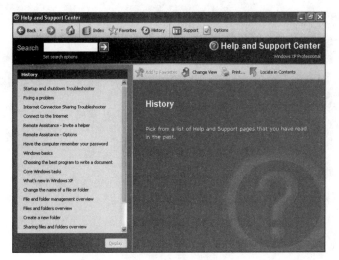

FIGURE 9-3

The History bar.

- Clicking Support displays a screen that describes the various ways you can get online and personal support for Windows XP. I'll discuss these choices in detail later in this chapter.
- Clicking Options opens a screen that you can use to define settings and configure Help And Support Center. I'll discuss those options in the next section.

As you can see in Figure 9-1, the home page is divided into four sections:

- Pick A Help Topic
- Ask For Assistance
- Pick A Task
- Did You Know?

To access the topics in the Pick A Help Topic section, click a link to open a page that contains content relevant to that topic and links to related material. For example, if you click the Windows Basics link, you'll see the page shown in Figure 9-4 (next page). Click a link in the pane on the left to open that topic in the pane on the right and in most cases to display a list of subtopics. Notice that when you point to a link on the home page, you'll see a pop-up box with an explanation of that link. For example, when you point to Windows Basics, the pop-up displays "Learn the ABCs of using Windows."

9

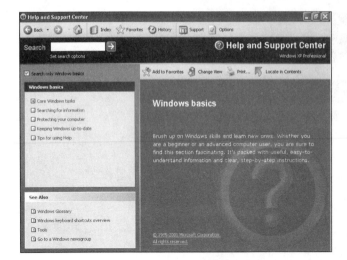

FIGURE 9-4

Opening a topic in Help And Support Center.

One of the most useful links in the Pick A Help Topic section is Fixing A Problem. When you click this link, you can access troubleshooters that step you through solving a number of problems. I'll discuss some of these troubleshooters in detail later in this chapter.

Clicking the links in the Ask For Assistance section open pages that you can use to get help via Remote Assistance, from Microsoft support experts, and from Internet newsgroups. I'll discuss how all three work later in this chapter.

The items in the Pick A Task section work as follows:

- If you are connected to the Internet, clicking Keep Your Computer Up-To-Date With Windows Update starts Windows Update, as discussed in Chapter 8.

- If you are connected to the Internet, clicking Find Compatible Hardware And Software For Windows XP opens a page at the Microsoft web site that lists products that have been tested and work with Windows XP.

- Clicking Undo Changes To Your Computer With System Restore starts System Restore, as discussed in Chapter 8.

- Clicking Use Tools To View Your Computer Information And Diagnose Problems opens the page shown in Figure 9-5. Clicking a link to one of these tools gives you the steps for using it. Chapter 8 looked at several of these tools in detail.

FIGURE 9-5

The Tools page in Help and Support Center.

Setting Help and Support Center Options

Clicking the Options button on the Standard toolbar displays the page shown in Figure 9-6.

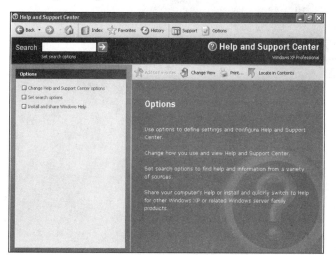

FIGURE 9-6

The Options page in Help and Support Center.

Click the Change Help And Support Center Options link to open the page shown in Figure 9-7. You use the check boxes and option buttons shown in Figure 9-7 to specify how you want to display items on the home page.

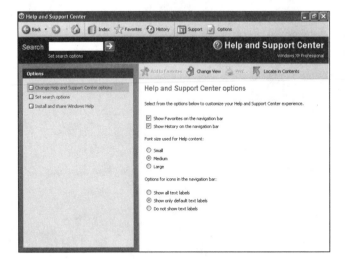

FIGURE 9-7

Options for changing the display of the home page.

Clicking the Set Search Options link opens the page shown in Figure 9-8.

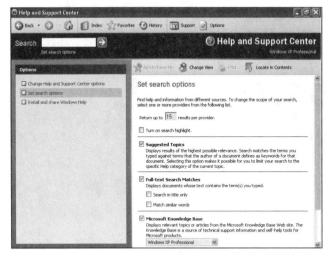

FIGURE 9-8

Setting search options.

You use these options to specify what happens when you search for a topic in Help and Support Center. By default, a search returns lists of items in three categories:

- Suggested Topics
- Full-Text Search Matches
- Microsoft Knowledge Base

Using the Set Search Options page, you can specify that you want results returned for all categories or only one or two. In the next section I'll discuss how these categories differ and when you might want to search one and not another. The first section on the Set Search Options page lets you tell Windows XP how many items to return in each category and whether to highlight the keywords on which you searched in found articles. The "searchlight" is not turned on by default. If you want to highlight terms, click the Turn On Search Highlight check box. Sometimes having terms highlighted is useful; at other times it's annoying. You might want to try this both ways to see which you prefer.

You'll see the third option, Install And Share Windows Help only if you have Windows XP Professional installed on your computer. Click this option if you want to install a help system for another operating system on your computer, for example, an XP server operating system.

Searching for Topics

I mentioned in the previous section that when you search, by default you could get results in three categories. Let's look at these categories and the kinds of information that each returns.

When a writer creates an article that appears in Help And Support Center, he or she specifies that certain words in that article are keywords. When you search on a term or phrase that matches the keywords in any articles, those articles appear in the Suggested Topics list, and they are, in the search engine's opinion, the articles that are most relevant to your search. Within the Suggested Topics list, articles are further categorized into a Pick A Task list and an Overview, Articles, And Tutorials list. You probably want to always keep the Suggested Topics list selected on the Set Search Options page.

The articles listed in the Full-Text Search Matches list contain at least one of the terms on which you searched. Consequently, these articles tend to be more peripheral to your topic. I tend to keep this option selected on the Set Search Options page because I have used this list to find important tidbits of information that, for whatever reason, did not turn up in any other way.

You may or may not find the articles listed in the Microsoft Knowledge Base helpful, and you will see articles listed here only if you are connected to the Internet at the time of your search. The Knowledge Base has been available on the Internet for some time (http://search.support.microsoft.com/kb/c.asp), and still is, but it has never before been

9

included with any Windows help system. In evaluating whether you want to include the Knowledge Base when you search, you may find it helpful to know how it evolved.

Early in Microsoft's history, you could actually call and speak to a support engineer over the telephone. As support engineers answered questions about Microsoft operating systems and applications and solved problems, they wrote up their findings. As you might imagine, over the years all of these articles began to constitute a vast database of information. It was and is now used by support engineers, and in various formats some of it has been published in book form. These articles vary widely in length, complexity, and technical content, ranging from the super simple to developer-level rocket science. You may seldom find anything of value to your situation in the Knowledge Base, and in that case you can save some time and bandwidth by not searching it every time you do a search. On the other hand, you never know what might turn up. I'd say, at the very least, take a look at some of these articles the next time you do a search, just so you know what's out there.

To display an article that appears in one of the results lists, click it to display its contents in the pane on the right.

Adding an Article to Your Favorites List

In Internet Explorer, you can place a web page on your Favorites list for quick and easy access, and you can do the same in Help And Support Center. To add the current page, simply click the Add To Favorites button. The page is added to your list, and Windows displays the message box shown in Figure 9-9 to let you know this.

FIGURE 9-9

Windows notifies you when it adds a page to your Favorites list.

To display a page on your Favorites list, click the Favorites button to display the Favorites bar, and then click the page to open it. To delete a page from the list, select it and click the Remove button. To rename a page, select it, click the Rename button, and then type the new name.

Changing the View

By default, Help And Support Center displays in full-screen view. You can, however, change to a reduced display. You might want to do this in particular when you are using one of the troubleshooters (discussed later in this chapter) so that you can see the steps and other windows on the screen. The earlier illustrations in this chapter all show Help And Support Center in full-screen view. To change to a reduced display, click the Change View button when displaying a topic. Figure 9-10 shows this reduced view. To change back to full-screen view, click the Change View button again.

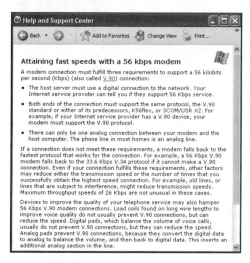

FIGURE 9-10

Help And Support Center in a reduced view.

Printing

To print a topic, click the Print button to open the Print dialog box. This is the same dialog box you see when printing from any Windows application. (See Chapter 4 if you need further information about printing.) The one feature you should know about is that instead of printing a single screen of help information, you can print an entire section of related topics. In the Print dialog box, click the Options tab, and then click the Print All Linked Documents check box. If you want to print a table of linked topics, click the Print Table Of Links check box.

Getting Support

To display the Support page in Help And Support Center, you can do one of the following:

- Click the Support button on the Standard toolbar.
- Click the Support link on the home page.

9

Whichever method you use, you'll see the Welcome To Support page shown in Figure 9-11.

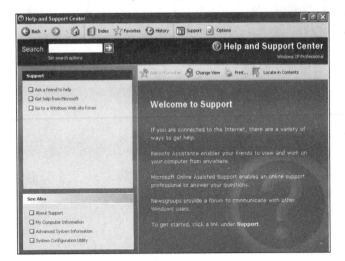

FIGURE 9-11

The Support page in Help And Support Center.

As you can see, you have three ways to access support: you can ask a friend or colleague for help, you can request help from Microsoft, and you can visit a newsgroup that discusses Windows topics.

Using Remote Assistance

Remote Assistance is a feature you can use to get help from a friend or colleague. Once your assistant's computer and your computer are connected, the two of you can chat via a box on the desktop, your assistant can see your desktop, and your assistant can even take control of your computer if you give them permission. As you might suspect, such an arrangement presents some security considerations, so you'll want to engage in such a setup only with a person you trust. Even then, you can't really tell if the person is who they say they are—someone could have hijacked their identity and password. The bottom line is that you need to be on the alert while using Remote Assistance and be prepared to take back control of your computer at any time.

With that caveat in mind, using Remote Assistance can be a definite help when you're having difficulty with a task or with your system and a knowledgeable friend or colleague is unable to be at your side. Remote, by the way, doesn't necessarily mean half way around the world; it just means not in your same physical location. The person could be in an office on another floor of your building or across town.

When you install Windows XP, Remote Assistance is enabled by default. To verify that this is the case, follow these steps:

1 Click the Start button, right-click My Computer, and choose Properties from the short-cut menu to open the System Properties dialog box.

2 Click the Remote tab, which is shown in Figure 9-12.

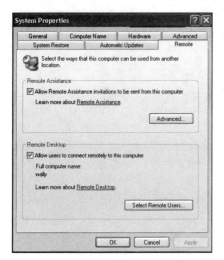

FIGURE 9-12

The System Properties dialog box, open at the Remote tab.

3 Verify that the All Remote Assistance Invitations To Be Sent From This Computer check box is checked. If not, select it.

4 Click OK.

Now you want to take care of one more task before you issue or respond to an invitation. You want to set some limits concerning whether your computer can be controlled remotely and the length of time a person has to respond to your request for help. To do so, follow these steps:

1 On the Remote tab of the System Properties dialog box, click the Advanced button to open the Remote Assistance Settings dialog box, as shown in Figure 9-13.

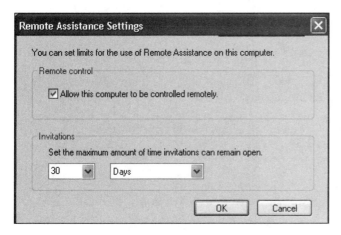

FIGURE 9-13

The Remote Assistance Settings dialog box.

2 If you don't want to allow remote control of your computer, be sure that the Allow The Computer To Be Controlled Remotely check box is cleared.

3 By default, the period of time during which a request for help can remain open is 30 days. For security reasons, you should shorten this period considerably.

4 Click OK.

To use Remote Assistance, both you and your assistant must be running Windows XP, and both must be connected to the Internet or connected to the same local area network.

Note If either you or your assistant works at a computer that is behind a firewall, check with your network administrator for further instructions.

You send an invitation requesting remote assistance either via Windows Messenger or e-mail. Let's look first at issuing an invitation through Windows Messenger and then at sending an e-mail invitation.

To send a Windows Messenger invitation, follow these steps:

1 Click the Start button, click All Programs, and then click Windows Messenger to start Windows Messenger.

2 Click the Tools menu, and then click Ask For Remote Assistance to open the Ask For Remote Assistance dialog box, as shown in Figure 9-14.

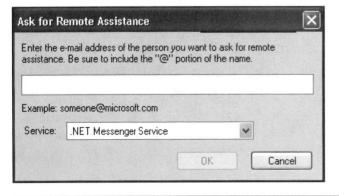

FIGURE 9-14

Enter the e-mail address of the person whose help you are requesting.

Note You can also right-click a contact's name and choose Ask For Remote Assistance from the shortcut menu.

3 Enter the person's e-mail address, and click OK.

4 Windows Messenger displays a message saying that your invitation is being sent.

To send an e-mail invitation, follow these steps:

1 On the Help And Support Center home page, click the Invite A Fried To Connect To Your Computer With Remote Assistance link in the Ask For Assistance section to open Remote Assistance, as shown in Figure 9-15.

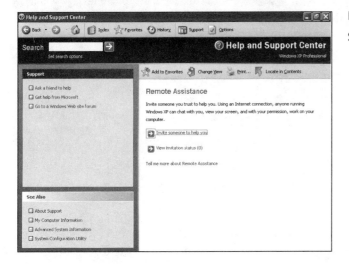

FIGURE 9-15

Starting Remote Assistance.

2 Click the Invite Someone To Help You link to open the screen shown in Figure 9-16.

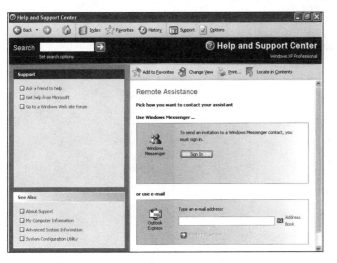

FIGURE 9-16

Select a contact method.

3 In the Or Use E-mail section, enter the address of your assistant or select if from your Address Book, and then click Invite This Person to open the screen shown in Figure 9-17.

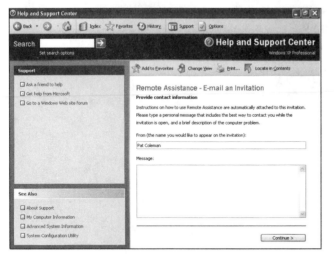

FIGURE 9-17

You can include a personal message with the invitation.

4 Optionally, in the Message box, type a personal note that describes your computer problem and any other information you want to convey, and then click Continue to open the screen shown in Figure 9-18.

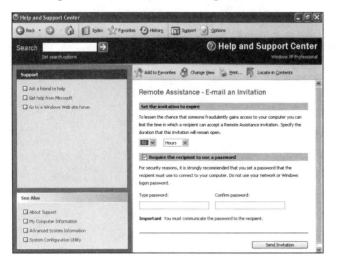

FIGURE 9-18

Set expiration time and a password.

5 Use the drop-down list boxes to set an expiration time for your invitation, and then supply a password and confirm it. Although setting a password is not required, it is strongly recommended for security reasons. You'll need to communicate the password to your recipient by some other means, perhaps a phone call or a separate e-mail. Click Send Invitation.

Your invitation is now sent, and it will include the instructions your recipient will need to connect to your computer. When the recipient clicks the filename in the Attach line, a dialog box opens in which the recipient can enter the password and connect to your computer.

Getting Help from Microsoft

When you use Microsoft Online Support, you can automatically collect information about your computer and submit it to Microsoft electronically. A Microsoft technical support person then sends you a solution that appears as a pop-up message in the notification area. Click the pop-up message to read the response in a Help And Support Center window.

To use Microsoft Online Support, you need to be connected to the Internet and you need a Microsoft Passport or Hotmail account. If you don't have one, Help And Support Center steps you through the process. To connect to Microsoft Online Support, click the Get Help From Microsoft link in the Support pane of the Support page. Now follow the onscreen instructions.

Using Windows Newsgroups

You saw in Chapter 5 that you can use Outlook Express to read Internet newsgroups. From Help And Support Center, you can access special newsgroups that are devoted to Windows XP topics. In the Support pane on the Support page, click Go To A Windows Web Site Forum to open the Windows Newsgroups page, as shown in Figure 9-19.

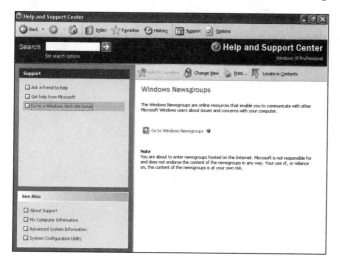

FIGURE 9-19

The Windows Newsgroups page in Help And Support Center.

9

Now follow these steps to read the postings in a newsgroup:

1 Click the Go To Windows Newsgroups link to open the Windows XP Newsgroups site, as shown in Figure 9-20.

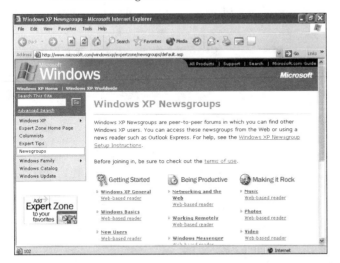

FIGURE 9-20

The Windows XP Newsgroups site.

2 Click a newsgroup to open its postings in Outlook Express, as shown in Figure 9-21.

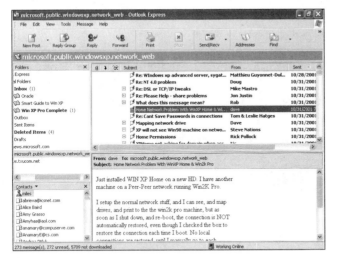

FIGURE 9-21

Opening a newsgroup in Outlook Express.

3 To read a posting, click its heading.

Note For more information about how to read and post to newsgroups in Outlook Express, see Chapter 5.

Using the Troubleshooters

A Windows XP troubleshooter is a guide in question-and-answer format that you can use to solve a problem you're having with hardware or software. You can access a troubleshooter in a couple of ways. First, Windows XP may detect a problem and ask you if you want to run a troubleshooter. Second, you can select a troubleshooter from Help And Support Center.

In this section, I'll use as an example that I'm having startup and shutdown problems. Follow these steps to use a troubleshooter that focuses on this particular problem:

1 On the home page of Help And Support Center, click the Fixing A Problem link to open the Fixing A Problem page shown in Figure 9-22.

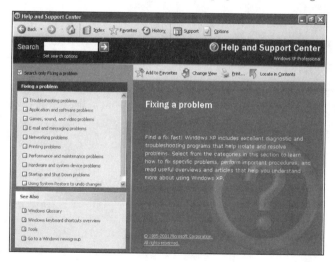

FIGURE 9-22

The Fixing A Problem page in Help And Support Center.

2 In the Fixing A Problem pane, click the Startup And Shutdown Problems link to open the Startup And Shut Down Problems page shown in Figure 9-23.

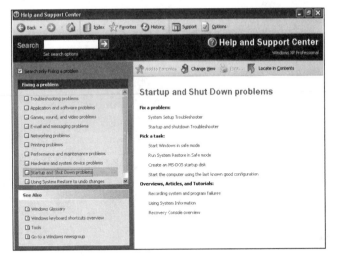

FIGURE 9-23

The Startup And Shut Down Problems page in Help And Support Center.

3 Click a problem, a task, or an article. In this example, if you click the Startup And Shutdown Troubleshooter link, you'll see the page shown in Figure 9-24.

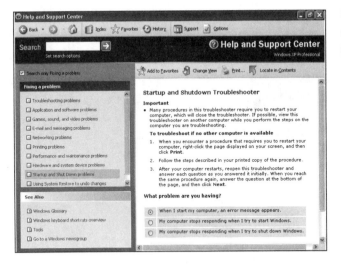

FIGURE 9-24

Using the Startup And Shut Down troubleshooter.

4 In this particular case, the troubleshooter advises you to view the troubleshooter on another computer while attempting to solve your problem. If that isn't possible, you can always print out the steps. When you use other troubleshooters, it's often possible to display the troubleshooter screen in reduced view while following its steps in other windows. Once you've tried a step, the troubleshooter will ask if the problem has been solved. If it has not you have the option of starting over, skipping the step, or trying something else.

Getting Help on the Internet

When you're troubleshooting a problem on your computer, don't overlook the sites of hardware and software manufacturers. They may offer fixes, suggestions, new drivers, and the like. You may even be able to send e-mail to a technical support person.

9

Chapter 10

Customizing Windows XP

When you first install Microsoft Windows XP, the Setup program configures your desktop, keyboard, and mouse according to a standard plan. For example, the keyboard is set for U.S. English, a short repeat delay, a medium repeat rate, and a medium-fast cursor blink rate. You can, however, customize the way that Windows works, and this chapter describes how to do the following tasks:

- Customizing the Taskbar and the Start Menu
- Using Control Panel
- Customizing your display
- Customizing your mouse
- Customizing the keyboard
- Adding and removing programs
- Adding new hardware to your system

To make all these changes and many others, you use the Control Panel, and I'll spend most of this chapter working with Control Panel. Before getting into that though, I first want to show you how to customize the taskbar and the Start menu.

Customizing the Taskbar and the Start Menu

As you know, the taskbar is located at the bottom of the desktop by default. At the far right of the taskbar is the notification area. When Windows XP is first installed, the taskbar is locked, that is, you can't move it or resize it. And unless your computer came with Windows XP installed when you bought it, probably the only thing you'll see on the taskbar is the time in the notification area. If you've used previous versions of Windows, you may recall that at the left side of the taskbar was an area called Quick Launch toolbar, which contained icons that you could click to open Internet Explorer and Outlook Express, and an icon that let you quickly show the desktop. The Quick Launch toolbar is not displayed in Windows XP by default, but you can choose to display it, as you'll see shortly.

When you open any program in Windows XP, an icon for every instance of that program is displayed on the taskbar. If the number of icons exceeds the available space, the taskbar displays a drop-down list that includes related items. For example, if you open a WordPad docu-

10

ment and then open yet another WordPad document, the task bar might display a drop-down list that includes the names of both documents. You click the drop-down list on the taskbar to display a particular item.

Customizing the Taskbar

If you want to be able to move and resize the taskbar, the first thing you'll need to do is unlock it. Simply right-click an empty area of the taskbar, and in the shortcut menu that appears, click Lock The Taskbar to remove the check mark. Now to resize the taskbar, point to its upper border. When the cursor becomes a double-pointed arrow, drag to reduce or increase the vertical width of the taskbar. To reposition the taskbar, click it in an open space and then drag to an edge of the screen. The taskbar snaps to that position. For example, if you click and drag to the right edge of the screen, the task bar becomes vertical instead of horizontal and runs along the right edge of the desktop.

To further customize the taskbar, you use the Taskbar And Start Menu Properties dialog box, which is shown in Figure 10-1.

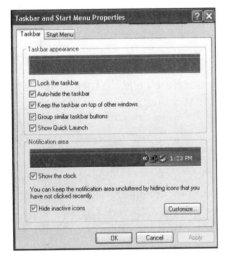

FIGURE 10-1

The Taskbar And Start Menu Properties dialog box, open at the Taskbar tab.

Using the check boxes on the Taskbar tab, you can do the following:

- Select Lock The Taskbar if you want users of your computer not to be able to move or resize the taskbar.
- Select Auto-Hide The Taskbar if you want the taskbar hidden until you move the pointer to the bottom edge of the desktop. You might want to select this option if you've increased the size of the taskbar and you need more of the screen available for use with various windows.

- Select Keep The Taskbar On Top Of Other Windows if you always want the taskbar to appear on the screen.
- Select Similar Taskbar Buttons if you want to group related items in a list, as described earlier.
- Select Show Quick Launch if you want to display the Quick Launch toolbar. If you then want to add an item to the Quick Launch toolbar, drag it from its position on the desktop or in the Start menu or other menu that you can see.

You can choose not to display the clock in the notification area by clearing the Show The Clock check box. In addition to the clock, the notification area displays icons that notify you of an event or an alert. For example, you can choose to display a You Have New Mail notification when you receive new e-mail. By default, Windows continues to display notification icons unless you don't use them, and then Windows hides icons for inactive items. You can, however, choose how you want items in the notification area to behave. To do so, follow these steps:

1 In the Taskbar tab of the Taskbar And Start Menu Properties dialog box, click the Customize button to open the Customize Notifications dialog box, which is shown in Figure 10-2.

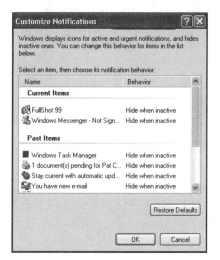

FIGURE 10-2

The Customize Notifications dialog box.

2 Select the item whose behavior you want to change from the Name list.

3 The items description in the Behavior column becomes a drop-down list box that contains the following behaviors:
- Hide When Inactive
- Always Hide
- Always Show

4 Select a behavior, and then click OK.

To restore the default behaviors, click the Restore Defaults button.

Customizing the Start Menu

As you know, the Start menu in Windows XP works differently from the Start menu in previous versions of Windows. If you prefer the classic Start menu, you can choose to use that, but you can also customize the Start menu in several other ways. To do so, you use the items on the Start Menu tab in the Taskbar And Start Menu Properties dialog box, which is shown in Figure 10-3.

FIGURE 10-3

The Taskbar And Start Menu Properties dialog box, open at the Start Menu tab.

If you prefer to use the Classic Start menu, click the Classic Start Menu option button. Figure 10-4 shows the Classic Start menu, and Figure 10-5 shows the Windows XP default Start menu.

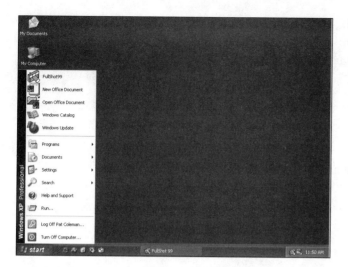

FIGURE 10-4

The Classic Start menu.

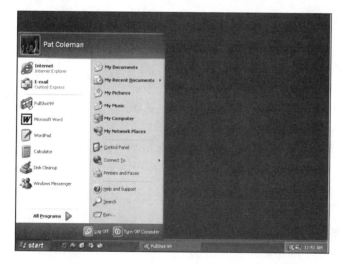

FIGURE 10-5

The Windows XP default Start menu.

10

You can customize both the Windows XP default Start menu and the Classic Start menu. To customize the Windows XP default Start menu, be sure that the Start Menu option button is selected, and then click the Customize button to open the Customize Start Menu dialog box, which is shown in Figure 10-6.

FIGURE 10-6

The Customize Start Menu dialog box for customizing the Windows XP default Start menu.

Figure 10-6 shows the Customize Start Menu dialog box open at the General tab. Follow these steps to select options in this tab:

1 In the Select An Icon Size For Programs, click either Large Icons or Small Icons. By default, items on the Start menu are displayed in Large Icons size.

2 In the Programs section, click the Number Of Programs On Start Menu drop-down list to select how many programs will be displayed. You can choose from none to a maximum of nine.

3 In the Show On Start Menu section, select whether you want to display an Internet or an e-mail program, and then click the drop-down lists to select the specific program. By default, the Start menu displays Internet Explorer as the Internet program and displays Outlook Express as the e-mail program. But you might want to change this display if you, for example, install another browser or a different e-mail program. If you install Outlook (part of the Microsoft Office suite of applications) after you install Windows XP, Outlook will become the default e-mail program. If you prefer Outlook Express, you can change back to that using the E-mail drop-down list.

To customize other Start menu items, click the Advanced tab, which is shown in Figure 10-7.

FIGURE 10-7

The Customize Start Menu dialog box, open at the Advanced tab.

Follow these steps to select options on the Advanced tab:

1 In the Start Menu Settings section, you can specify that submenus display when you click an item rather than point to it by clearing the Open Submenus When I Pause On Them With My Mouse check box.

2 By default, the Highlight Newly Installed Programs check box is selected. Therefore, when you install any new program it and all its components are highlighted on the Start menu. This highlighting continues to be displayed for what seems to me a rather long period. In fact, I find this annoying, so I clear this check box. After all, if you've installed new programs, you know that you have done so, and each one appears on the All Programs menu. However, if several people use your computer, using the highlight could certainly be helpful in notifying them when others have installed new programs.

3 You can use the Start Menu Items list to customize items in a number of ways. Scroll down this list to see the options. Check those that you want to enable.

4 To include a My Recent Documents item on the Start menu, be sure that the List My Most Recently Opened Documents check box is selected. Then, to open a recently accessed document, click My Recent Documents, and select the document from the submenu. The document opens in the program in which it was created.

5 Click OK.

10

Note If you choose to use the Classic menu and want to customize it, click the Customize button to open the Customize Classic Start Menu dialog box and use its options. If you've previous versions of Windows, you'll know how to do this, so I won't go into this topic here.

Using Control Panel

In Windows XP Professional, Control Panel is available in two views: Category View and Classic View. The default view is Category View, which is shown in Figure 10-8. To open Control Panel, you click the Start button and then click Control Panel.

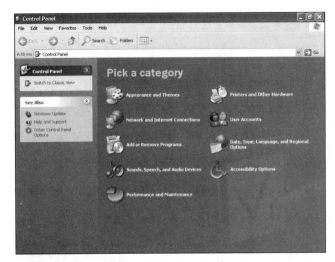

FIGURE 10-8

Control Panel in Category View.

If you've used previous versions of Windows, you may find this view of Control Panel puzzling. It's not immediately obvious which applets are in which category, and to open an applet, you must first select the category and then select the applet. Table 10-1 shows what you'll find in each category.

Category	Contents
Appearance and Themes	Taskbar and Start Menu
	Folder Options
	Display
Network and Internet Connections	Network Connections
	Internet Options
Add or Remove Programs	Opens the Add Or Remove Programs dialog box
Sounds, Speech, and Audio Devices	Sounds and Audio Devices
	Speech
Performance and Maintenance	Administrative Tools
	Scheduled Tasks
	System
	Power Options
Printers and Other Hardware	Printers and Faxes
	Scanners and Cameras
	Game Controllers
	Mouse
	Keyboard
	Phone and Modem Options
User Accounts	Opens the User Accounts folder
Date, Time, Language, and Regional Options	Regional and Language Options
	Date and Time
Accessibility Options	Accessibility Options

Table 10-1: Category contents in Control Panel.

The category folder, in many cases, also contains a list of tasks that are related to the applets in that category.

Notice that on the left of Control Panel in Category View is a See Also bar that contains links to Windows Update and Help and Support. If you are connected to the Internet, clicking Windows Update takes you to the Microsoft Windows Update site at *http://windowsupdate.microsoft.com/*. Clicking Help And Support opens Help and Support Services.

10

If you don't find Category View to your liking, you can switch to Classic View of Control Panel, which is shown in Figure 10-9. To do so, click the Switch to Classic View link in the Control Panel bar.

FIGURE 10-9

Control Panel in Classic View.

Figure 10-9 shows Control Panel in Classic View and in Icons view. You can also display the Classic View in Thumbnails, Tiles, List, and Details view. Click the View menu, and then choose a view. Notice that in Classic View you also have the See Also bar that contains Windows Update and Help and Support links.

Note If you are an experienced user you'll probably want to work with Control Panel in Classic View. In this chapter, though, for the sake of consistency, illustrations and steps will reflect Category View.

Now let's put Control Panel to work and use it to customize Windows.

Customizing Your Display

First let's deal with the settings that change the appearance of your desktop most obviously. To take a look at your options (and to change them if you want), you use the Display Properties dialog box, which you can open in a couple of ways:

- Right-click an empty area on the desktop, and choose Properties from the shortcut menu.
- Click the Start button, click Control Panel, click Appearance And Themes, and then click Display.

Figure 10-10 shows the Display Properties dialog box open at the Themes tab.

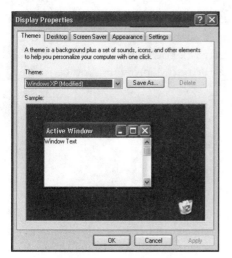

FIGURE 10-10

The Themes tab of the Display Properties dialog box.

Specifying a Theme

In Windows XP, a theme is a group settings that all together give the desktop a certain look. These settings include the desktop background, colors, font styles and sizes, window sizes, sound events, mouse pointers, icons, and even a screen saver. When you apply a theme, you change the way Windows XP looks. To apply a theme, follow these steps:

1 In the Themes tab, click the drop-down Theme list box.

2 Choose one of the listed themes, or click Browse to find a theme you've stored on your computer.

3 You'll also find more themes online. If you are connected to the Internet, click More Themes Online to go to the Microsoft Plus! For Windows page. Click the Themes link to open the Plus! Themes page, from which you can buy Microsoft Plus! For Windows, which contains a selection of themes.

4 Click OK if you simply want to apply a selected theme. If you want to modify it in some way, such as choose a different background, click Apply. When you made the modifications in the other tabs in the Display Properties dialog box, click the Themes tab again, and then click Save As to save the theme you've created.

Customizing the Desktop

You use the settings in the Desktop tab (see Figure 10-11) to determine the display behind the icons on your desktop and to further customize the desktop. For the background, you can use the graphic files you have on your computer, you can use artwork you've downloaded from the Internet, or you can use any of several backgrounds that Windows provides. You can also choose a color for the background.

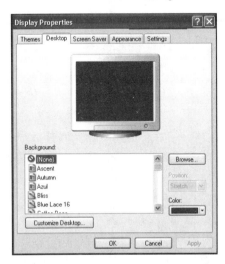

FIGURE 10-11

The Display Properties dialog box, open at the Desktop tab.

To get a sense of the possibilities, follow these steps:

1 In the Background list, click the down arrow to scroll down and select a background.

2 Initially, your selection is tiled, as you can see in the display area. To view it in other ways, click the down arrow in the Position box. Choosing Center places the background in a square frame in the center of your screen, and choosing Stretch fills the entire screen.

3 When the background is to your liking, click the Apply button and then click the OK button.

Note To select a file on your system as the background, click the Browse button.

If you don't want to display a picture as the background, choose None. You can then click the Color drop-down list and select a color as the background.

To further customize the desktop, click the Customize Desktop button to open the Desktop Items dialog box, which is shown in Figure 10-12.

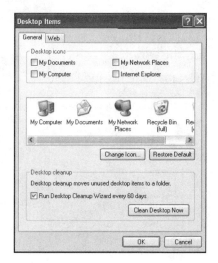

FIGURE 10-12

The Desktop Items dialog box, open at the General tab.

On a clean install of Windows XP (see the Appendix for how to install Windows XP), you'll see only a single desktop icon—the Recycle Bin. (If you bought your computer with Windows XP already installed, your computer manufacturer may have already placed several icons on your desktop.) If you want to display other items on the desktop, you can drag them there, or you can use the Desktop Icons section of the General tab. To display an item click its check box. If you want to change the item's icon, click Change Icon to open the Change Icon dialog box, which is shown in Figure 10-13.

FIGURE 10-13

The Change Icon dialog box.

To substitute an icon displayed in the Change Icon box for the original icon, select it from the list, and click OK. If you want to use an icon stored on your system, click the Browse button.

At the bottom of the Desktop Items is the Run Desktop Cleanup Wizard Every 60 Days check box, which is selected by default. When this wizard runs, it removes any unused items on the desktop. You can also click the Clean Desktop Now button to run the wizard.

If you want to display a web page on your desktop, click the Web tab, which is shown in Figure 10-14.

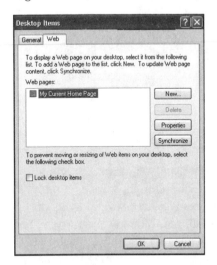

FIGURE 10-14

The Desktop Items dialog box, open at the Web tab.

To simply display your home page on your desktop, click the My Current Home Page check box, and then click OK. You can, however, customize how, when, and where a web page is displayed using the many options available in this tab. For information about how to do this, look in Help And Support Center.

Choosing a Screen Saver

A screen saver is a program that displays either a completely black image or a constantly changing image after a computer has been idle for a preset amount of time. The original purpose of a screen saver was to prevent a stationary image from "burning" into the phosphor of the screen. These days there is no risk of burning an image into your screen display, but people still use screen savers to make a personal statement and for their entertainment value.

Note A lot of screen savers are available on the Internet, and you can often download them for free. I would caution you against doing so. Screen savers are notorious virus transportation systems. In addition, people who lack the basic skills for developing a program to run under Windows often create them. Consequently, they can cause other software to malfunction and crash your computer.

Using the Screen Saver tab of the Display Properties dialog box (see Figure 10-15), you can select a screen saver of your choice, password-protect it if you want, and establish the amount of time that your computer is idle before the screen saver starts up.

FIGURE 10-15

The Screen Saver tab of the Display Properties dialog box.

Let's select one of the screen savers that comes with Windows and play with the settings to see how this works. To select a screen saver, follow these steps:

1 In the Screen Saver section of the Screen Saver tab, click the down arrow and select a screen saver from the list. You'll see a small preview in the display area.

2 To see what this screen saver looks like in Full Screen view, click the Preview button. You'll see the screen saver in action for a second or two. Jiggle the mouse to see the Display Properties dialog box again.

3 To customize the screen saver, click the Settings button to open the Settings dialog box (see Figure 10-16 on the next page) for the selected screen saver. Figure 10-16 shows the Settings dialog box for the Marquee screen saver. The displayed settings depend on the screen saver you chose.

10

FIGURE 10-16

The settings for the Marquee screen saver.

4 Click OK or Apply when you're happy with the settings.

To specify the period of inactivity after which the screen saver kicks in, select a number of minutes in the Wait *x* Minutes spin box. If you want to protect your system with the screen saver, apply a password. In this way, only someone who knows the password can close the screen saver and access the files on your system. When you click the On Resume, Password Protect check box, you or anyone else must enter your log on password to get past the screen saver.

If you scroll down the items in the Screen Saver list, you'll see the My Pictures Slideshow item. You can select this item to use any photos or other art stored on you computer as a screen saver slideshow. To do so follow these steps:

I Place the pictures you want in the slideshow in a convenient folder. The default is to use the My Pictures folder in your Documents and Settings folder, but you can use any folder you want.

2 Select the My Pictures Slideshow screen saver, and then click Settings to open the My Pictures Screen Saver Options dialog box, which is shown in Figure 10-17.

FIGURE 10-17

The My Pictures Screen Saver Options dialog box.

3 Drag the slider to specify how often pictures should change and how big they should be.

4 If you haven't placed the pictures in your My Pictures folder, click Browse to open the Browse for Folder dialog box. Locate the folder, and then click OK to close the Browse For Folder dialog box.

5 Select your options in the lower section of the My Pictures Screen Saver Options dialog box, and then click OK.

Note It's best to clear the Use Transition Effects Between Pictures check box. The transitions detract from the pictures themselves.

---

6 Back in the Screen Saver tab of the Display Properties dialog box, click the Preview button to see if you like the settings you've specified. If you're satisfied with them, specify the Wait time and whether to apply a password, and then click OK. If you aren't satisfied, open the My Pictures Screen Saver Options dialog box again, and change them.

Conserving Power

If energy efficiency is important to you (or to your company), you can set your computer to go on standby, and you can set your monitor and/or hard disk to turn off after one minute of idle time, five hours of idle time, or several periods of time in between. In the Monitor section, click the Settings Power to open the Power Options Properties dialog box, as shown in Figure 10-18.

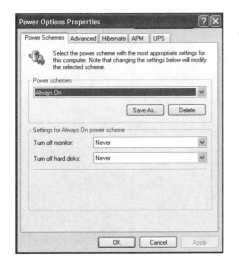

FIGURE 10-18

The Power Options Properties dialog box.

In the Power Schemes section, click the down arrow to choose a scheme that is appropriate to your situation. Then in the Settings For section, specify the amount of time after which you want your power scheme to go into effect.

Note When on standby, your monitor and hard disk turn off and your computer uses less power. When your computer comes out of standby, your desktop is restored exactly as you left it. Standby is particularly useful for saving battery power in portable computers.

When the power settings are to your liking, click the OK button to return to the Display Properties dialog box.

You use the other tabs in the Power Options Properties dialog box as follows:

- On the Advanced tab, click the Always Show Icon On The Taskbar check box if you want to display the icon. Click the Prompt For Password When Computer Resumes From Standby if you have selected the standby scheme and if you want anyone who then has access to your computer to supply your log on password before being able to use the computer.
- To enable hibernation, click that check box on the Hibernate tab.
- If your computer supports Advanced Power Management (APM), you will see an APM tab in the Power Options Properties dialog box. To enable APM, click the check box on the APM tab.
- If you have installed an Uninterruptible Power Supply (UPS) on your system, you can configure it using the UPS tab.

Note A UPS is a battery supplied power source that serves as a backup power supply in the event of an electrical power failure.

Customizing the Appearance of Windows and Dialog Boxes

Click the Appearance tab (see Figure 10-19) to apply your designer impulses to all sorts of Windows elements, including the following:

- Icons
- ToolTips
- Menus
- Message boxes
- Inactive title bars
- Caption buttons
- Window borders

FIGURE 10-19

The Display Properties dialog box, open at the Appearance tab.

The upper half of the dialog box displays the current style and color scheme. In the Windows And Buttons drop-down list, you can choose to display windows and dialog boxes in the Windows XP style or the Windows Classic style. To check out other color scheme possibilities, click the Color Scheme down arrow. Select a different color scheme, and you see its effects in the display area. You can also change the font size that is used for text in windows and dialog boxes. Click the Font Size drop-down arrow to choose from Normal, Large Fonts, or Extra Large Fonts.

To set the color scheme for a particular item, click the Advanced button to open the Advanced Appearance dialog box, which is shown in Figure 10-20. Click Item down arrow to select the item, and then select a size and color or colors. The font currently used for the item is displayed in the Font box. To select another font, choose its size, color, and emphasis (boldface or italic). When these settings are to your liking, click the Apply button.

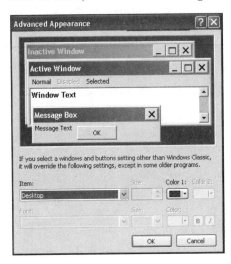

FIGURE 10-20

The Advanced Appearance dialog box.

> **Note** Unless you have a high tolerance for distraction, you don't want to get too wild and crazy here. However, you can experiment all you want, because you can always reset the appearance to something a little less stimulating.

Back in the Appearance tab, click the Effects button to open the Effects dialog box, which is shown in Figure 10-21. In this dialog box, you can select a check box to enable an option. Most of these items are self-explanatory, but I want to call your attention to the last check box, Hide Underlined Letters For All Keyboard Navigation Until I Press The Alt Key. If you tend to primarily use the keyboard instead of the mouse and this check box is selected, you may wonder why the keyboard shortcuts for menu commands and the like don't appear in a dialog box. Well, with this check box selected, you'll first need to press the Alt key and then press the Alt key combination. Clear this check box to avoid this extra key press. When you've made your selections in the Effects dialog box, click OK.

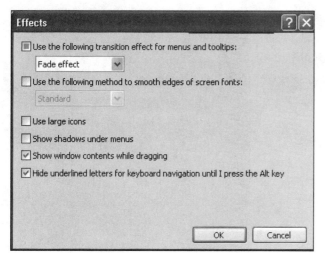

FIGURE 10-21

The Effects dialog box.

Changing the Screen Resolution and Number of Colors

Resolution is the number of pixels (dots) on the screen and the number of colors that can be displayed at the same time. The higher the resolution, the smaller elements appear on the screen. So if you have a small monitor, you'll want to stick with a lower resolution. Here are some common settings and the monitors on which they display best:

- 640 by 480 is a standard VGA (Video Graphics Adapter) display, which is quite readable for most people on a 15-inch monitor.
- 800 by 600 is a super VGA display. On a 15-inch monitor, this is really small, but it's quite readable on a 17-inch monitor.
- 1024 by 768 is the upper limit of super VGA, and it's readable on a 17-inch monitor.
- 1280 by 1024 is a resolution for very large monitors.

To change the screen resolution, you use the Settings tab in the Display Properties dialog box, which is shown in Figure 10-22.

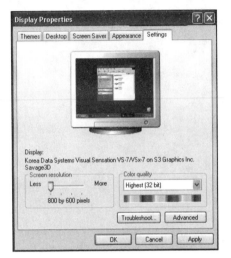

FIGURE 10-22

The Display Properties dialog box, open at the Settings tab.

To change the resolution, you simply move the slider on the Screen Resolution bar. The available choices depend on the size and type of your monitor, and only the recommended settings are displayed.

The maximum number of colors that can be displayed depends on your monitor and your display adapter. To see the available options, click the Color Quality drop-down list. To select a color quality click it.

Note If you are having difficulties with your display, click the Troubleshoot button to start the Video Display Troubleshooter in Help And Support Center.

To open a Properties dialog box for your monitor, click the Advanced button. Figure 10-23 shows this Properties box for my monitor. Ordinarily, you don't need to change any of the settings in this dialog box, but I will point out one setting that you need to know about if you change the screen resolution. Depending on which option is selected in the Compatibility section on the General tab, your computer might or might not reboot when you change the screen resolution. To specify what happens when you change the screen resolution, choose one of the three options in this section.

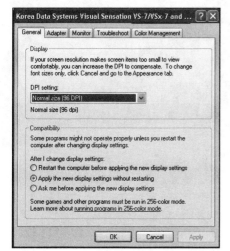

FIGURE 10-23

The Properties dialog box for a monitor.

Customizing Your Mouse

Personalizing your mouse can be extremely important if you're left-handed because, by default, the mouse is configured for use by the right hand. By using the Mouse Properties dialog box, you can also set the click speed, the size and shapes of pointers, and pointer speed and trail.

Note   If other people regularly use your computer, you may need to let them know when you change features such as standard icons and mouse behavior. Or you need to take advantage of User Profiles, which configure settings for multiple users. User Profiles are beyond the scope of this book, but if you work on a network, you can probably get additional information about how to use them from your network administrator.

To open the Mouse Properties dialog box, as shown in Figure 10-24 (next page), open Control Panel, click the Printers And Other Hardware link, and then click the Mouse link.

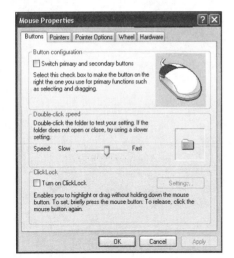

FIGURE 10-24

The Mouse Properties dialog box.

Obviously, you configure the mouse for left-handed use by selecting that option button in the Button Configuration section of this dialog box. To adjust the double-click speed, move the pointer on the slider bar. You'll see the speed change in the test area, so you can preview before you implement the change.

ClickLock is a feature that lets you select or drag without holding down the mouse button continuously. If you enable ClickLock (by checking the Turn On ClickLock check box), simply press and hold down a mouse button or a trackball button for a moment. You can then drag objects or make multiple selections, for example. When the operation is complete, click the mouse or trackball button again to release ClickLock. To decrease or increase the time you need to hold down a button before your click is locked, click the Settings button to open the Settings for ClickLock dialog box, which is shown in Figure 10-25.

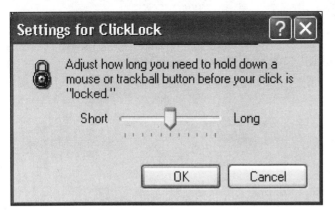

FIGURE 10-25

The Settings For ClickLock dialog box.

Move the slider, and then click OK. You'll probably want to experiment with this feature. If you find you don't like using it, simply clear the Turn On ClickLock check box.

Customizing Pointers

In the Mouse Properties dialog box, select the Pointers tab to display the list of available pointers, as shown in Figure 10-26. When you select a scheme, the pointers that make up that scheme are displayed in the lower portion of this dialog box.

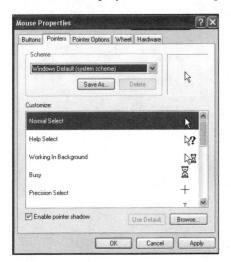

FIGURE 10-26

Personalize your mouse pointers using the Pointers tab.

To get an idea of your available choices, click the down arrow in the Scheme box. You'll see several schemes. To use one of these schemes, select it, click the Apply button, and then click the OK button.

> **Note**
>
> If you want to change one of these pointers to something that isn't available in the lists, click the Browse button and select the filename of a different pointer. If you don't see any pointers in the Browse dialog box, you can install optional mouse pointers by using the Add/Remove Programs tool in the Control Panel. (We'll look at this tool in the next section.)

Customizing the Speed and Trail of Your Pointer

To change the motion of your mouse pointer, select the Pointer Options tab, as shown in Figure 10-27.

FIGURE 10-27

The Mouse Properties dialog box, open at the Pointer Options tab.

By default, the speed of your pointer is set at about medium. To change the speed, move the slider toward Slow or Fast. Click the Apply button, and then click the OK button to test the speed.

If you want the pointer to automatically point to the default button when you open a dialog box, click the check box in the Snap To section.

Don't know what a pointer trail is? Select the Display Pointer Trails check box to find out. You can set the size of the trail by moving the slider toward Short or Long. To get back to your trailless pointer, click the Show Pointer Trails check box to clear it.

If you want the pointer hidden when you type, which is the default behavior, be sure that the Hide Pointer While Typing check box is selected. You can then select the Show Location Of Pointer When I Press The Ctrl Key check box to manually display the pointer whenever you want.

You use the other tabs in the Mouse Properties dialog box as follows:

- In the Wheel tab, you can specify how many lines are scrolled per wheel notch.
- If your mouse isn't behaving properly, click the Hardware tab, and then click Troubleshoot to start the Mouse Troubleshooter in Help And Support Center.

Customizing Your Keyboard

When you install Windows XP, the operating system recognizes your keyboard, and you don't normally need to tinker with the keyboard settings. You can, however, use the options in the Keyboard Properties dialog box, which is shown in Figure 10-28, to adjust the character repeat rate, to adjust the cursor blink rate, and to troubleshoot your keyboard.

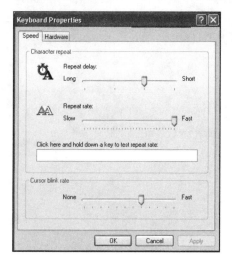

FIGURE 10-28

The Keyboard Properties dialog box.

To open the Keyboard Properties dialog box, in Control Panel click the Printers And Other Hardware link, and then click the Keyboard link. In the Speed tab, click the pointer on the slider bars to set the repeat delay, the repeat rate, and the cursor blink rate. The Hardware tab contains information about your keyboard. If you're having problems with your keyboard, click the Troubleshoot button to start the Keyboard Troubleshooter in Help And Support Center. Click the Properties button to display the Properties dialog box for your keyboard.

Adding and Removing Programs

To add and remove Windows applications and Windows components, you use the Add Or Remove Programs applet in Control Panel. To add an application that everyone on your system can use, you need to log on as a Computer Administrator. To add an application for a particular user on the system, log on with that person's user name.

Note   To add non-Windows programs, follow the instructions that are included with the application.

10

Adding a New Program

To add a new program, follow these steps:

1   In Control Panel, click the Add Or Remove Programs category, and then click the Add New Programs icon to open the Add Or Remove Programs dialog box, which is shown in Figure 10-29.

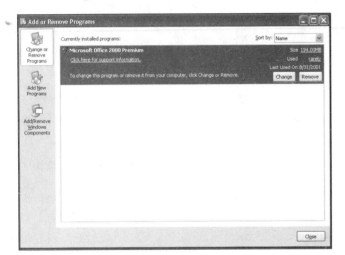

FIGURE 10-29

The Add Or Remove Programs dialog box.

2   Click the CD Or Floppy button. A wizard then guides you through installing and configuring the new application. Follow the onscreen instructions.

Note   If you are connected to the Internet, you can click the Windows Update button to go to a Microsoft Web site where you can download files for new Windows XP Professional features, system updates, and device drivers.

Changing and Removing Programs

From time to time, you will want to get rid of existing programs that you've installed, or change them. If you've been a long-time user of Windows, you may remember the day when you could simply locate the executable file for a program and delete it. The only safe way to remove a program in Windows XP Professional is to click the Change Or Remove Programs button in the Add Or Remove Programs dialog box, select the program you want to remove, and then click the Change/Remove button.

Adding and Removing Windows Components

To add or remove a Windows XP Professional component, you will need to be logged on as a Computer Administrator, and you will need your installation CD at hand to add components. Click Add/Remove Windows Components in the Add Or Remove Programs dialog box to start the Windows Components Wizard, as shown in Figure 10-30. To add or remove a component, follow the onscreen instructions.

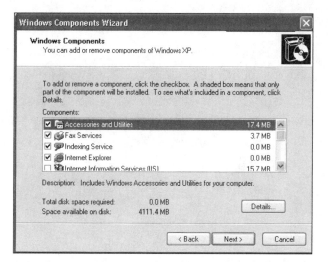

FIGURE 10-30

The Windows Components Wizard.

Adding New Hardware to Your System

Adding new hardware—such as a modem, an additional hard drive, or a CD-ROM drive—is really a snap with Windows XP. Most of today's hardware is designed to be Plug and Play. That is, you connect the hardware, and Windows takes care of the details concerning its device driver and any associated software. To install Plug-and-Play hardware on your system, follow these steps:

1 Turn off your computer, if necessary.

2 Connect the hardware according to the manufacturer's instructions.

3 Turn on your computer. Windows finds the new Plug-and-Play device and installs the necessary software.

Note   If you're adding a Universal Serial Bus (USB) or Firewire device, all you need to do is plug the device in and turn it on. You don't need to turn your computer off first.

If your new hardware is not Plug and Play, and the device came with an installation CD, follow the manufacturer's instructions to install the device. If the device did not come with a

CD or you don't have the CD, you'll need to use the Add Hardware Wizard (see Figure 10-31) to guide you through the process. This wizard makes the appropriate changes to the Registry and to the configuration files so that Windows can recognize and support your new hardware.

FIGURE 10-31

The first dialog box of the Add Hardware Wizard.

To install hardware that is not Plug and Play, follow these steps:

1 In Control Panel, click the Printers And Other Hardware category, and then in the See Also bar, click Add Hardware to start the Add Hardware Wizard.

2 Click the Next button.

3 Follow the on-screen instructions, which vary depending on the device you are installing.

Note You must log on as a Computer Administrator to run the Add Hardware Wizard.

Chapter 11

Entertainment, Sounds, and Games

Let me be honest right from the start: This was not an easy chapter to write, and that's certainly not because the concepts are difficult to grasp or because the skills are difficult to explain or master. To the contrary—the difficulty lay in exploring all the entertainment features now included with Microsoft Windows XP and then getting back to work!

Depending on the configuration of your computer system, you can use it for the following activities:

- Watching videos
- Playing audio CDs
- Making movies
- Recording audio
- Adding sounds to documents
- Attaching custom sounds to various Windows events
- Playing games

Using Media Player

Media Player plays and organizes digital sound and video files stored either on your computer or on the Internet. You can use Media Player to listen to Internet radio stations, watch videos and DVDs, listen to music CDs—and collect and store information about these items.

Because the version of Media Player in Windows XP supplies many new features and tools as compared with earlier versions, let's quickly review the Media Player window, which is shown in Figure 11-1. To open Media Player, click the Start button, point to All Programs, and then click Windows Media Player.

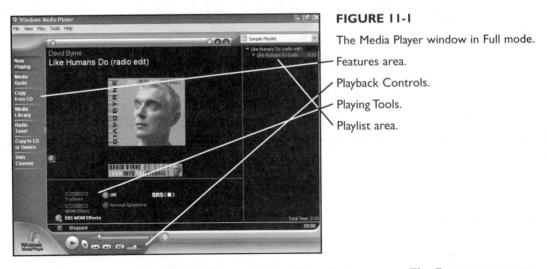

FIGURE 11-1

The Media Player window in Full mode.

Features area.

Playback Controls.

Playing Tools.

Playlist area.

Along the left edge of the Media Player window is the Features area. The Features area supplies the clickable tabs Now Playing, Media Guide, Copy From CD, Media Library, Radio Tuner, Copy To CD Or Device, and Skin Chooser. You use the Now Playing tab to play a CD, DVD, or video. The Media Guide retrieves information from the Internet. You use the Copy From CD tab to copy tracks from the music CD in your CD drive. You use the Media Library tab to see and maintain a list of the media files on your computer and the media hyperlinks that you've saved. You use the Radio Tuner tab to listen to an Internet radio station. Click the Copy To CD Or Device tab to see a list of storage devices (such as recordable and rewriteable CDs) that you can use for copying music to CDs. Click the Skin Chooser tab to display a list of looks you can choose for the Media Player window.

Along the bottom edge of the Media Player window are the Playback Controls. These controls, which I'll briefly describe in the next section "Playing DVDs and CDs," let you play, pause, adjust the volume, fast forward, and rewind a video, CD, or DVD.

Just above the Playback Controls is the Playing Tools area. This area provides options for adjusting the equalization, choosing a video quality, selecting a DVD playback speed, and so on.

Along the right edge of the Media Player window is the Playlist area. The Playlist area displays a list of the items you can play or watch. If you've inserted a music CD in the CD drive, for example, the Playlist area lists the music tracks. If you've inserted a DVD, the Playlist area lists the chapters. If you've indicated you want to listen to an Internet radio station, the Playlist area lists the radio stations on the Presets list (which is just a list of memorized radio stations).

Playing DVDs and CDs

To play a music CD or watch a DVD, insert the CD or DVD in your CD or DVD drive. Windows XP starts Media Player and opens the Media Player window shown in Figure 11-2.

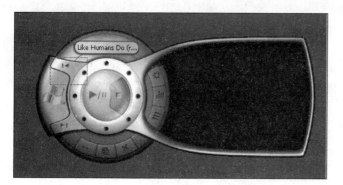

FIGURE 11-2

The Media Player window in Skin mode.

> **Note** Media Player lets you work with two versions of the Media Player window: Full mode, shown in Figure 11-1, and Skin mode, shown in Figure 11-2. To switch between these two modes, click the View menu and click Full Mode or Skin Mode.

Using Media Player to listen to a music CD or watch a DVD is very easy. The Media Player window provides buttons and controls that mimic those available on the typical CD player or DVD player:

- To start the CD or DVD, click the Play/Pause button. To pause the music, click the Play/Pause button again.
- To stop the CD or DVD, click the Stop button.
- To move ahead or back to a track or chapter, click the Previous or Next buttons.
- To skip ahead or back up, click the Rewind or Fast Forward buttons.
- To adjust the volume, drag the Volume slider.

Note You can also use the Play menu's commands to specify how a music CD or DVD should play. Most of the commands on the Play menu correspond to buttons described in the preceding list. Only three new commands, in fact, appear: Shuffle, which randomly plays tracks on the music CD; Repeat, which tells Media Player to repeat playing a track; and Eject, which ejects the music CD or DVD from the CD or DVD drive.

Note Media Player includes visualizations (sometimes called skins) of the music that you can watch as you listen to a music CD. To display a visualization, click the View menu and click Visualization. When Media Player displays the Visualization submenu, choose a visualization theme from the first submenu and then a visualization effect from the second submenu. A picture in a book doesn't do justice to the visualizations, so you'll want to experiment with visualizations yourself to see how they work.

Note The Media Player window also includes buttons for working with visualization effects: Click the Select Visualization button to display a menu of visualization themes. To try the next or previous visualization effect, click the Next Visualization or Previous Visualization button.

Click the View menu, click Now Playing Tools, and then click Show Equalizer And Settings to add controls to Media Player for adjusting the equalization of the music and for displaying additional information about the music CD or DVD you're playing, as shown in Figure 11-3.

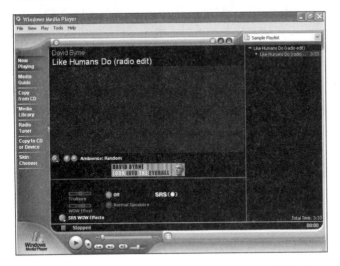

FIGURE 11-3

The Media Player window with the Equalizer and Setting controls.

Media Player supplies six sets of Equalizer and Setting controls:

- SRS WOW Effects, shown in Figure 11-3, lets you turn on and off the surround sound (SRS) effect, select a speaker size, and adjust the bass and WOW effect.
- Graphic Equalizer lets you adjust the equalization of the music by dragging slider but-

tons. The Graphic Equalizer controls also include a button for selecting equalizer settings appropriate to different styles of music: jazz, rock, swing, opera, and so on.

- Video Settings provides slider buttons you can use to adjust the Brightness, Contrast, Hue, and Saturation of the video played by Media Player.
- Media Information displays information about the CD, DVD, or video you're playing.
- Captions displays captions for a video when this information is available.
- Lyrics displays the words of a song when this information is available.
- DVD Controls provides a slider button for adjusting the play speed of the DVD and a button for moving to the next frame of the DVD.

The View menu's DVD Features command displays a submenu of commands you can use to work with DVDs.

- Capture Image takes a picture of the current frame's image and places the picture on the Windows Clipboard.
- Subtitles And Closed Captions displays a menu with two commands: Closed Captions and Subtitles. Click Closed Captions to add closed captioning to the DVD (if captioning is available). Click Subtitles and then select a language if you want to see subtitles in another language.
- Audio And Language Tracks displays a list of the languages in which you can hear a DVD's or a movie's soundtrack.
- Camera Angle lets you choose the angle from which you want to view the DVD.

Playlists list media items you can play or watch. For example, a playlist can list tracks on a music CD or identify video clips stored on your local drive.

To create a playlist, follow these steps:

1 Click the Media Library tab, and then click the New Playlist button as shown in Figure 11-4. When Media Player displays the New Playlist dialog box, name the new playlist by entering a name in the box shown in Figure 11-5.

FIGURE 11-4

The Media Library tab.

FIGURE 11-5

The New Playlist dialog box.

2 Select the items you want to add to the playlist by clicking them. To select multiple items, hold down the Ctrl key as you click.

3 Click the Add To Playlist button. When Media Player displays a list of the available playlists, click the playlist to which the selected items should be added.

You can edit the list of items on a playlist. To add a new item to the playlist, display the Media Library, right-click the item you want to add, choose Add to Playlist from the shortcut menu, and then select the playlist to which you want to add the item. To remove an item on the playlist, click the Media Library tab, click the playlist you want to change, right-click the item you want to remove, and choose Delete From Playlist from the shortcut menu.

To play the items in a playlist, select the playlist from the Playlist box. The Playlist box appears in the upper right corner of the Media Player window.

If your computer includes a writeable or recordable CD drive, you can create your own music CDs. To do so, follow these steps:

1 Insert the music CD in the CD drive, and then click the Copy From CD button in the Features area to see a list of the tracks on the CD shown in Figure 11-6. Next, check the tracks you want to copy to the Media Library, and then click the Copy Music button. Media Player begins copying the selected tracks to the Media Library. This step may take several minutes.

FIGURE 11-6

The Copy From CD tab.

Note To stop copying a track, click the Stop Copy button. The Stop Copy button replaces the Copy Music button when Media Player is copying tracks.

---

2 Click the Media Library tab, open the track's folder, and then select the tracks that you want. To copy more than one track, hold down the Ctrl key as you click the tracks.

3 Click the File menu, and click Copy To CD Or Device. When Media Player displays a list of the storage devices to which you can copy music tracks, select the CD drive. Then click Copy Music.

Note If you click the Tools menu, click Options, and then click the Copy Music tab, Media Player displays a tab of options you can use to specify how Media Player copies the music. The Copy Music tab, for example, lets you specify where copied music is stored, choose a file format, and select a music quality setting.

Listening to Internet Radio Stations

Media Player allows you to find and listen to Internet radio stations. To locate an Internet radio station, click the Radio Tuner tab in the Features area shown in Figure 11-7. You can double-click one of the stations listed in the Presets box. Or you can use the Station Finder boxes to provide search criteria for building a list of stations; click Search, and then double-click one of the stations your search returns.

FIGURE 11-7

The Radio Tuner.

Note   To add a new station to the list of Presets, click the station and then click the Add The Station You Have Selected To Your Preset List button. To delete a station from your list of Presets, click the station and then click the Delete A Station From Your Preset List button.

Using Movie Maker

Movie Maker creates movies by piecing together video-clip files stored on your computer or on the Internet, video clips you shoot with a home video or camera, and narration you record with a microphone. Once you've created your movie, you can store the movie as a file on your computer, send the movie file in an e-mail message, or post the movie file to a Web server. You and anyone else can then view the movie using Media Player.

Setting Up a Movie Project

To set up a movie project, start the Movie Maker accessory by clicking the Start button, clicking All Programs, clicking Accessories, and then clicking Windows Movie Maker, as shown in

Figure 11-8. After you start Movie Maker, create a movie project file for the new movie by clicking the File menu, clicking New, and then clicking Project.

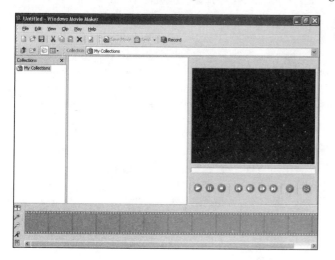

FIGURE 11-8

The Movie Maker window.

Collecting Video Clips

After you set up a movie project, you collect video clips for your movie. You can collect video clips from a digital video camera or by importing video-clip files stored on your computer.

To collect video clips from a digital video camera, click the File menu and click Record. After Movie Maker opens the Record dialog box, select Video from the Record list box shown in Figure 11-9. You can use the Record Time Limit box to specify how long a video clip you want to record. Then click Record, and play the video on your digital camera. Movie Maker adds video clips to the clip area.

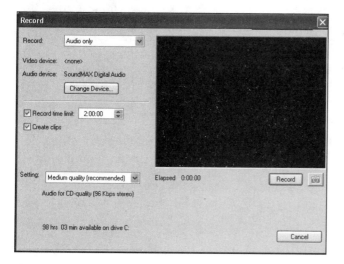

FIGURE 11-9

The Record dialog box.

To add a video clip stored on your computer, click the File menu and then click Import. When Movie Maker opens the Select The File To Import dialog box, use the Look In and File Name boxes to identify the video-clip location and file, as shown in Figure 11-10. Click Open. Movie Maker adds video clips to the Movie Maker clip area.

FIGURE 11-10

The Select The File To Import dialog box.

Working with Clips

To create your movie, you arrange the clips in a sequence. To do this, drag a clip from the clip area to the movie frame area at the bottom of the Movie Maker window. Arrange the clips in the same order as you want to play them.

Note You can rename a clip by clicking its name twice and then typing a new name.

To play a clip, click the clip to select it and then click the Play button.

If you want to use only part of a clip, you can split the clip into two clips by clicking the clip, playing the clip until the frame where you want to split the clip, and then clicking the Split Clip button.

> **Note** You can use the Next Frame and Previous Frame buttons to move one frame at a time through the clip.

You can combine two clips into a single clip by selecting the clips, right-clicking the selected clips, and then choosing Combine from the shortcut menu.

You can play your sequence of movie clips by right-clicking the storyboard and choosing Play Entire Storyboard/Timeline from the shortcut menu.

Adding Narration

You can add narration to a movie. Click the View menu, and click Timeline to add a timeline to the storyboard pane. Then click the File menu, and click Record Narration. Movie Maker displays the Record Narration Track dialog box shown in Figure 11-11.

FIGURE 11-11

The Record Narration Track dialog box.

To begin recording, click the Record button and then narrate the movie. When you finish, click Stop. When Movie Maker displays the Save Narration Track Sound File dialog box, name the sound file and click Save, as shown in Figure 11-12 (next page). Movie Maker saves your sound file as a WAV file and imports the file into the open movie project.

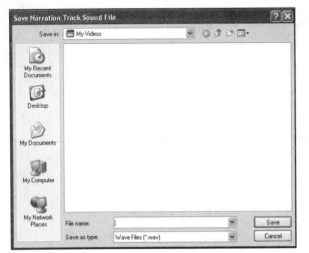

FIGURE 11-12

The Save Narration Track Sound File dialog box.

Saving a Movie

After you arrange your clips and add any sound, you can save your movie by clicking the File menu and clicking Save Movie. When Movie Maker displays the Save Movie dialog box, use the Setting box to pick a movie quality. Then, as appropriate, describe the movie using the Title, Author, Date, Rating, and Description boxes shown in Figure 11-13. Click OK when you finish providing this information.

FIGURE 11-13

The Save Movie dialog box.

When Movie Maker displays the Save As dialog box, specify where the movie should be saved using the Save In box, pick a format for the movie using the Save File As Type box, and name the movie using the File Name box shown in Figure 11-14.

FIGURE 11-14

The Save As dialog box.

Note Movie Maker takes several minutes to create your movie.

Playing the Movie

You play movies using Media Player. To do this, click the File menu and click Open to open the movie file. Then click the Play button. To view your movie in a full-screen window, click the View menu and click Full Screen.

Using the Sound Recorder

If you're fortunate enough to have all the right equipment, you can use the Sound Recorder to make your own voice recordings or record from another sound source. To make voice recordings, you need a microphone and a sound card, and to play back what you recorded, you need speakers. To record sounds from another device such as an audio CD or a stereo receiver, you'll need a Line In connector to your sound card.

Note Once you create a voice recording, you can insert that file into documents and send them to others. Of course, the recipients also need the appropriate equipment to play your recording.

To open Sound Recorder, which is shown in Figure 11-15, click the Start button, point to All Programs, Accessories, and Entertainment, and then click Sound Recorder.

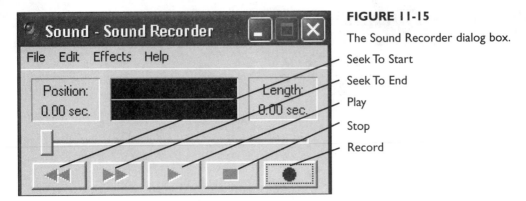

FIGURE 11-15

The Sound Recorder dialog box.

Seek To Start

Seek To End

Play

Stop

Record

At the bottom of the Sound Recorder dialog box are the buttons you use to control Sound Recorder. Here's what they do:

- Seek To Start moves to the beginning of a sound file.
- Seek To End moves to the end of a sound file.
- Play plays the sound.
- Stop halts playing or recording.
- Record begins recording.

If you want to make a voice recording and you have all the necessary equipment, follow these steps:

1 Open Sound Recorder.

2 Choose the File menu's New command.

3 Turn on your microphone.

4 Choose the File menu's Properties command. Windows displays the Properties For Sound dialog box.

5 Choose Recording Formats from the Choose From drop-down menu. Then click the Convert Now button. Windows displays the Sound Selection dialog box.

6 Choose quality for the sound from the Name drop-down menu—CD Quality, Radio Quality, or Telephone Quality. Then click OK, and click OK again in the Properties For Sound dialog box.

7 Click the Record button, and then speak into your microphone.

8 When you're finished, click Stop.

9 Choose the File menu's Save As command to save your voice recording as a file.

When you're creating a sound track, the Position indicator displays your location on the track, and the Length indicator displays the current length of the sound track. The slider moves to give you a visual impression of your position. The green line in the visual display gives you hints as to the quality of the sound.

If you want to insert your sound track into a document, choose the Edit menu's Copy command. Then, in the document, click the Paste command.

Associating Sounds with Windows Events

When you install Windows XP, certain sounds are associated with particular events (of course, you need a sound card and speakers to hear them). You can choose to retain these sounds, you can change them, or you can silence them altogether. To do any of this, you use the Sounds applet in the Control Panel. Click the Start button, and then click Control Panel. Click the Sounds, Speech, and Audio Devices link to open the Sounds And Audio Device Properties dialog box, and then click the Sounds tab, which is shown in Figure 11-16.

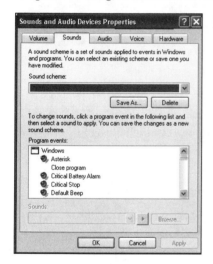

FIGURE 11-16

The Sounds And Audio Devices Properties dialog box, open at the Sounds tab.

Silencing Your Computer

If you want peace and quiet while working at your computer, follow these steps:

1 In the Sound Scheme drop-down list box, select No Sounds.

2 Click the OK button.

That's it—no more dings, trills, whistles, or heavenly chords.

Changing the Sound for a Single Event

If you want to change the sound associated with a particular event, follow these steps:

1 In the Program Events list, select the event. (You'll see the name of the current sound file associated with the event in the Sounds drop-down list.)

2 Click the Browse button to open the Browse For *Event* Sound dialog box with the Media folder selected, as shown in Figure 11-17.

FIGURE 11-17

The Browse For *Event* Sound dialog box.

3 Select the sound file you want. You can preview the sounds by clicking the Play Sound button at the bottom of the dialog box. If you like the new sound, click the OK button.

4 If you want to keep the sound for the event, click the Save As button to open the Save Scheme As dialog box, as shown in Figure 11-18.

FIGURE 11-18

The Save Scheme As dialog box.

5 Type a name for the sound scheme, and then click the OK button.

Playing Games

If you need convincing, a quick trip to your local software emporium will attest to the enormous popularity of computer games. Some games are incredibly complex and can take over your life if you let them. You can also download games from many web sites. Your easiest access to some computer games that many find just as intriguing as those you can buy or download is through Windows. For several years now, Windows has included four games: FreeCell, Hearts, Minesweeper, Solitaire, and Pinball. In this section, we'll look at how to play these games, explain the rules, and give you some tips for winning. Windows XP also includes access to games that you can play over the Internet. In the last part of this chapter, I'll describe those.

To open a game in Windows XP, click the Start button, point to All Programs, and then click Games to see a submenu of games.

Solitaire

Solitaire is the American name given to a number of card games that can be played by one person. The English name for the game is Patience. The object of the game is to build four complete suit stacks, each containing all the cards of one suit, in order, from ace through king.

As Figure 11-19 shows, the first hand is dealt for you when you open Solitaire. To deal a new game after you complete one, choose the Game menu's Deal command.

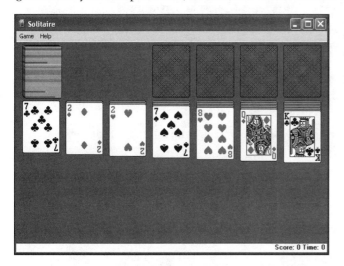

FIGURE 11-19

The first Solitaire hand is dealt for you when you open the game.

Note   You can choose from among 12 decks of cards. Choose the Game menu's Deck command, select a deck, and then click the OK button.

Your first order of business after a hand is dealt is to move any aces that are face up to the spaces at the upper right of the screen and then turn over the cards that were underneath the aces. (To display a face down card, simply click it.)

Next, check to see if you can make any plays on the piles. You must play black cards (spades and clubs) on red cards (hearts and diamonds) and red cards on black cards in descending order. For example, you can play the queen of diamonds on the king of clubs, but you cannot play the queen of spades on the king of clubs. One pile can be moved in its entirety to another pile, if its bottom card can be played on the other pile's top card.

Note To move a card or a stack of cards, drag it.

When you have made all available plays on the piles, click the deck to turn over the first three cards; only the top card is displayed. If you can play it on a pile, do so; if not, click the deck again. Continue clicking the deck and making plays. Whenever you free an ace, move it to the space at the top and then, as you uncover the appropriate cards, build on the aces in sequence from ace through king.

When you click completely through the deck, click the deck space to start over. You win when all the piles are empty and each of the four aces is built up completely. When you win, Windows rewards you with a little graphical surprise. If you run through all the cards in the deck without being able to play any of them, the game is over, and you lose.

Note By default, Windows uses a Standard scoring system for Solitaire. To use another scoring system, choose the Game menu's Options command and choose from among Standard, Vegas, and None. You can also choose to turn over one card at a time from the deck instead of three.

I make no claim that any of the following tips will ensure your winning at Solitaire, but they will increase the odds:

- Take a good look at all the possible moves before you click the deck.
- If you have a choice, play cards on the piles instead of moving them to ace stacks. This ensures that you'll uncover all the cards in the piles sooner.
- When a pile is empty, you can place a king in it, either from another pile or from the deck.
- You can always choose the Game menu's Undo command to reverse the last move.

Note If you're a real Solitaire enthusiast, you might want to try your hand at Spider Solitaire, which uses two decks of cards. Click Help to read the rules.

FreeCell

Unlike Solitaire, it is believed (though not proven) that it is possible to win every game of FreeCell. (Now that's a reason to have lunch at your desk.) Like Solitaire, in FreeCell you lay out a tableau of cards and then attempt to arrange them in their respective suits. The object of FreeCell is to move all the cards to the home cells, stacked by suits in order from ace through king.

Open FreeCell, and choose the Game menu's New Game command to deal a hand, as shown in Figure 11-20.

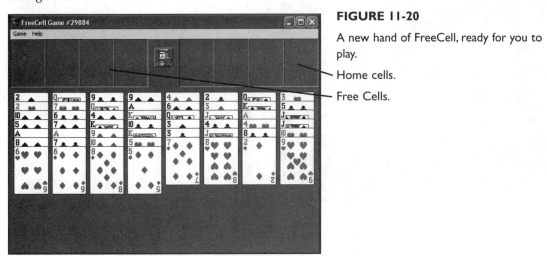

FIGURE 11-20

A new hand of FreeCell, ready for you to play.

Home cells.

Free Cells.

As you can see in Figure 11-20, the four free cells are in the upper left, and the four home cells are in the upper right. Before you make a move, locate the aces and the lower cards, especially twos and threes. If you are lucky enough to have some aces at the bottom of columns, click them first and then click a home cell to move them into it.

Here are your basic moves:

- You can move the bottom card of a column to a free cell or to a home cell.
- You can move the bottom card of a column to another column if it follows in sequence. That is, you can place a red jack on a black queen, a black four on a red five, and so on.
- You can move a sequence of cards from one column to another if the other column has enough free space. To do so, click the top card of the sequence and then click the bottom of the column where you want to move it. (You'll see a warning message if there is not enough free space.)
- You can move a card from a free cell to a home cell or to the bottom of a column if it follows in sequence.

- You can move any card to an empty column.

You probably won't get the hang of FreeCell instantly, but I predict that it won't take more than a half hour or so to win your first game. If you start a game and think you're stuck (which happens frequently at first), you can start that game over by choosing the Game menu's Restart Game command. Figure 11-21 shows a game of FreeCell in progress.

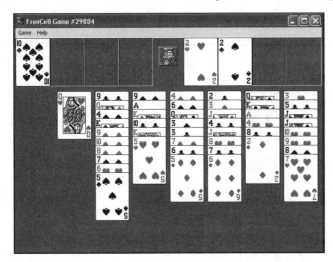

FIGURE 11-21

A game of FreeCell in progress.

You have at your disposal 32,000 different hands of FreeCell. When you choose the Game menu's New Game command, FreeCell selects a game at random. To select a particular game, choose the Game menu's Select Game command and then enter a game number.

Note   If you share your computer, be aware that anyone can check up on your FreeCell play. Choose the Game menu's Statistics command to display a report on games played, games won and lost, and so on.

After you play FreeCell for awhile, you'll discover your own tricks for rooting out deeply embedded aces and the like. In the meantime, here are some strategies to get you started:

- Try to keep at least one free cell open.
- Aim to get empty columns whenever you can. These can be more valuable than free cells because you can add cards in sequence.
- To reveal the suit of a partially hidden card, right-click it.
- When only one legal move remains, you'll see a warning on the title bar.

Note   To minimize a game at any time (for example, when the vice-president of your company pops into your office unannounced), press the Esc key.

Hearts

Hearts is so-called because every card of the heart suit counts against you when won in tricks. This, of course, is the opposite of such related games as Bridge, and indeed, the 18th-century ancestor of Hearts was called Reverse. As Antony says in *Julius Caesar*, "I come not, friends, to steal away your hearts."

When you start Hearts, you'll see The Microsoft Hearts Network dialog box (see Figure 11-22) if you are connected to a network. (If you are not connected, you won't see this dialog box.)

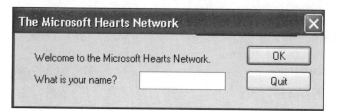

FIGURE 11-22

The Microsoft Hearts Network dialog box.

The object of Hearts is to collect as few tricks as possible that contain hearts and thereby have the lowest score at the end of the game. At the end of a hand, you get 1 point for each heart in your pile of tricks and 13 points if you have the queen of spades. The game continues until one player gets 100 points. If you win all the hearts and the queen of spades in one hand (called Shooting the Moon), you get no points, and each of the other players gets 26 points.

Figure 11-23 shows how the screen looks when the hands have been dealt for a new game. (The cards are dealt as soon as you close the Microsoft Hearts Network dialog box.) As you can see, your cards are face up, and the cards of the other players are face down.

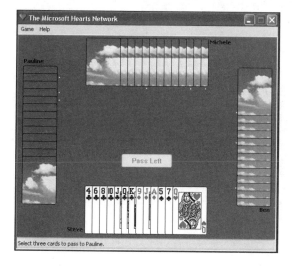

FIGURE 11-23

A new game of Hearts is about to begin.

Each player first passes three cards to the player on the left, except for the fourth hand when no cards are passed. The player with the two of clubs leads it first. Each player in turn must play a card, following suit if possible. In any case, you cannot play a heart or the queen of spades on the first trick. The person who plays the highest card of the suit that was led takes the trick and then leads another card. You cannot lead a heart until a heart has been played on a previous trick. Play continues until all 13 tricks have been taken.

Note To change the speed of the animation, rename the players, and turn sound on or off, choose the Game menu's Options command and then use the Hearts Options dialog box.

Winning at Hearts is a matter of skill and practice, and of course, you can get all the practice you have time for since you can play against the computer. The following list of guidelines will help get your strategy off on the right foot.

- If you're dealt the ace, king, and queen of spades, don't pass the ace and king. You can often use these cards to take a trick that you'd otherwise have to take with the queen of spades.

- Try not to take any tricks that contain the queen of spades or hearts (unless you're trying to Shoot the Moon or prevent someone else from doing so).

- Try to get rid of the queen of spades first and as soon as possible; you can then worry about getting rid of hearts.

- If you think another player is trying to Shoot the Moon, attempt to take a trick that contains at least one heart.

- Try early on to get rid of all the cards in one suit. When you have a void (as this is called), you can then play any other suits when the void suit is led.

Minesweeper

The games we've looked at so far are electronic versions of card games you may well have played as a child or with your grandmother. Minesweeper, on the other hand, is not a derivative. It is strictly a computer game, and it has to do with deduction and logic. The object of Minesweeper is to uncover all the squares in a minefield that don't contain mines and to mark the squares that do contain mines as quickly as possible. (I prefer to not think about any real-world analogy to this game.)

When you start Minesweeper, you'll see a grid like that shown in Figure 11-24.

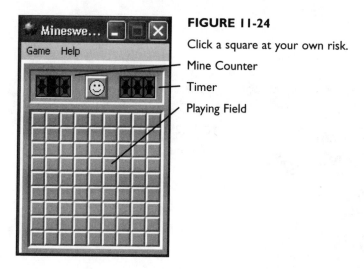

FIGURE 11-24

Click a square at your own risk.

Mine Counter

Timer

Playing Field

To begin, click any square to uncover it. Now, there are two possibilities:

- The square could be blank, indicating that no mines are in the surrounding squares.
- The square could contain a number, indicating how many mines are in the surrounding squares.

When you click the second square, however, there is a third possibility: the square could contain a mine, in which case all mines are displayed and you lose.

The Mine Counter shows the number of unmarked mines in the field, and the Timer shows the time elapsed since you uncovered the first square.

If you think a square contains a mine, right-click it to mark it. If you just aren't sure about a square, right-click it twice to put a question mark in it. If you later want to uncover the square, click it again.

By default, Minesweeper is set for a beginning level of play. To increase the difficulty, choose the Game menu's Intermediate, Expert, or Custom commands. The number of grid squares increases with each succeeding level of difficulty.

Minesweeper is not an easy game to win, but here some tips to get you going until you develop a strategy of your own:

- If a square contains the number 1 and only one uncovered square is next to it, that square must contain a mine.
- After you mark all mines around a numbered square, click that square with both mouse buttons to quickly uncover all empty squares around it.
- Keep an eye out for common number patterns. These often indicate a corresponding pattern of mines.

Pinball

Space Cadet 3D Pinball is the electronic version of the pinball machines found in a typical arcade. Unlike the other Windows games, Pinball is played with the keyboard. The object is to launch the ball and earn lots of points by hitting bumpers, targets, and flags. You begin each game with three balls and at the rank of Cadet. Figure 11-25 shows a game in progress.

FIGURE 11-25

A game of Pinball in progress.

Playing Internet Games

If you are connected to the Internet, you can play games over a games server, including Backgammon, Checkers, Hearts, Reversi, and Spades. For purposes of a quick example, we'll look briefly at playing Internet Checkers. Figure 11-26 shows a game about to begin.

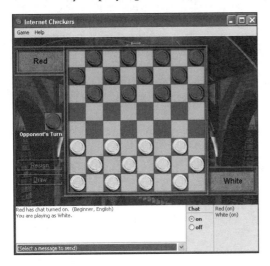

FIGURE 11-26

An Internet game of Checkers about to begin.

To move a checker, click it and then drag it. To make a jump, simply drag your checker over that of the other player. When a checker is in position to be "kinged," it will display a crown. Chat is turned on by default, and you click the drop-down arrow to select a message to send. To select a skill level for the game, click the Game menu, and then choose from Beginner, Intermediate, or Expert.

For information on how to play any Internet game, click the Help menu.

Note You'll find many game sites on the Internet. For starters, search on "game sites."

Appendix

Installing Windows XP

Installing Windows XP is not particularly difficult, but the process is more involved than installing previous versions of Windows and requires some preparation. In this appendix, I'm not going to walk you through the actual installation step by step; Windows XP provides a Setup wizard that will do that. In addition, the steps vary depending on the type of installation you choose. I will walk you through the steps to take before you install, and I'll explain the types of installation.

System Requirements

Your first task before attempting to install Windows XP is to verify that your computer system can run Windows XP. Using the tools that I discussed in earlier chapters, verify that your computer system meets or exceeds the following requirements:

- A minimum of a Pentium II processor running at 233MHz, but a 600MHz or faster processor will provide much better performance.
- At least 64MB of RAM, but 128MB of RAM is preferred. Windows XP can access a maximum of 4GB of RAM.
- At least 650MB of free disk space on a 2GB hard drive; more if you are installing over a network. In reality, you'll want at least 1GB of free disk space, as well as room for your applications and files.
- A video adapter and monitor capable of 800 by 600 screen resolution.
- A CD or DVD drive.

Verifying System Compatibility

Windows XP helps you with this task by providing the Upgrade Advisor. The Upgrade Advisor takes a look at your system and then displays a report. To run the Upgrade Advisor, follow these steps:

1 Insert your Windows XP CD in the CD drive.
2 At the Welcome screen, which is shown in Figure A-1, click the Check System Compatibility link.

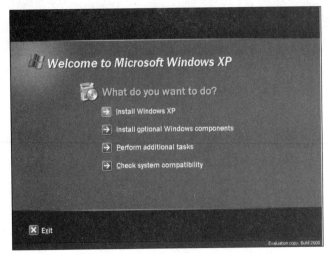

FIGURE A-1

At the Welcome screen, click the Check System Compatibility link.

3 On the next screen, click the Check My System Automatically link.

4 If you are connected to the Internet, the Upgrade Advisor offers to run Dynamic Update to download any updated Setup files from the Windows Update site. To skip this step or if you are not connected to the Internet, click the No, Skip This Step And Continue Installing Windows option button.

5 The Upgrade Advisor then scans your system and presents its report. Figure A-2 shows an example of a report that has found no problems. If the Upgrade Advisor does find problems, click the Full Details button to take a look at the details and find advice on what to do about the problems.

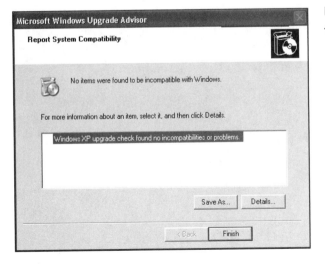

FIGURE A-2

The Upgrade Advisor's report.

6 Click Finish.

Choosing an Installation Type

If you've verified that your computer system is capable of running Windows XP, you next need to decide the type of installation you will do. Here are your choices:

- Upgrade. An upgrade overwrites the version of Windows currently installed and transfers all your files, settings and applications. You can upgrade if you are currently running Windows 95 or any version of Windows 98, Windows NT Workstation (including service packs), or Windows 2000 Professional (including service packs).

- New installation. A new installation replaces the version of Windows currently installed. You can also do a new installation on a clean hard drive or a separate partition. You can use the Files and Settings Transfer Wizard to copy your files and settings from your current system. (I'll explain how to run the Files and Settings Transfer Wizard in the next section.)

- Clean installation. A clean installation sets up Windows XP from scratch and does not upgrade from the version your are currently running. You'll need to reinstall your applications after doing a clean install of Windows XP. You can use the Files and Settings Transfer Wizard to copy your files and settings. If you are installing Windows XP on a new partition or a new hard drive, you'll need to do a clean install.

Choosing a File System

During the installation of Windows XP, you will be asked to choose a file system. A file system in an operating system is the overall structure that determines how files are named, stored, and organized. You can choose from the following three systems:

- FAT, which stands for File Allocation Table and is the file system supported by DOS, Windows 3.*x*, and Windows 95 release 1 (16-bit operating systems).

- FAT32, which stands for File Allocation Table 32 and is the file system supported by Windows 95 release 2 and Windows 98 (a 32-bit operating system).

- NTFS, which stands for New Technology File System and is the file system supported by Windows NT and Windows 2000.

Which you choose depends in part on the size of your hard drive, how you plan to set up your network (if you intend to network your computers), and how secure you want your system to be.

Note A 16-bit operating system can work with 2 bytes, or 16 bits, of information at one time. A 32-bit operating system can work with 4 bytes, or 32 bits, of information at one time.

The FAT File System

The FAT approach to organizing your files is to create a database (the File Allocation Table) at the beginning of your hard drive. When you store a file on your hard drive, the operating system places information about it in the FAT so that you can later retrieve the file when you want it. You cannot use the FAT file system with a disk larger than 2.6 gigabytes. The FAT file system uses the 8.3 file-naming convention; that is, a file's name can be a maximum of eight letters. The three letters following the period are the file extension, which identifies the file's type. If you have a computer that uses the FAT file system and is connected via a network to a computer that uses the NTFS file system, you will not be able to see the files on the NTFS computer. The FAT file system does not provide any security.

The FAT32 File System

The FAT32 file system evolved from the FAT file system, but because of the way it is structured, you can use FAT32 with a hard drive as large as 2 terabytes. FAT32 also uses space on your hard drive much more efficiently. In addition, the FAT32 system lets you use long filenames; the maximum is 255 characters. The FAT32 file system is, therefore, a much better choice that FAT, but it sill can't see the files on an NTFS system, and it does not provide any security.

The NTFS File System

Although you can use the FAT and FAT32 file systems with Windows XP, Microsoft recommends that you use NTFS for the following reasons:

- It has many security features, including password protection for files and folders.
- It provides better disk compression and files encryption (if you are running Windows XP Professional). In other words, you can store more in less space, and you can encode data to prevent unauthorized access.
- You can use NTFS on a hard drive as large as 2 terabytes, and performance does not degrade as drive size increases.
- It provides better protection from viruses. Most viruses are written to attack systems formatted to FAT and FAT 32, and they don't know what to do when they encounter NTFS.
- NTFS creates a backup of the Master File Table (MFT), which is the equivalent of the FAT database. If the boot sector of your hard drive becomes damaged, you can replace the information from that backup.
- NTFS includes features required for hosting Active Directory, so if your network uses Active Directory, you have to choose NTFS.

Note A Windows XP installation that uses NTFS can see and access FAT and FAT32 files.

Which File System Is Best for You?

No one file system is best in all situations, so here are some guidelines:

- If you are installing Windows XP on a standalone system or on a network that includes only Windows XP machines, go with NTFS. NTFS is a robust, secure file system, and though it causes the operating system to run a bit slower that it would using FAT32, it is your best bet if you want the additional features.

- If you are setting up a network that will be accessed by DOS, Windows 3.x and/or Windows 95/98/Me machines, consider using FAT. Remember that FAT and FAT32 can't see NTFS files.

- If you are setting up a dual-boot configuration, for example, one partition uses Windows 98 and the other uses Windows XP, and it is important that each operating system be able to see the other's files, use FAT or FAT32.

Running the Files and Settings Transfer Wizard

Before you start the Files and Settings Transfer Wizard, be sure that you have plenty of storage on the medium you'll use to place the data while you are installing Windows XP. Although you can save setting files to a floppy disk, a floppy won't be sufficient for holding all your data files. Copying to a CD is ideal, although you can also store files on a network drive.

To use the Files and Settings Transfer Wizard to copy your files and settings to another medium, follow these steps:

1 Insert your Windows XP CD in the CD drive.

2 At the Welcome screen, which is shown earlier in Figure A-1, click the Transfer Files And Settings link.

At the Welcome To The Files And Settings Transfer Wizard screen, click Next to open the Which Computer Is This? screen, as shown in Figure A-3.

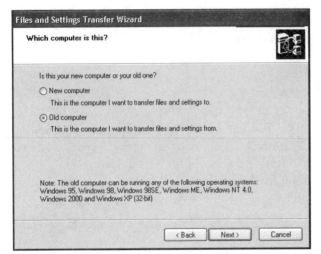

FIGURE A-3

Identifying the computer.

Click the Old Computer option button, and then click Next to open the Select A Transfer Method screen, as shown in Figure A-4.

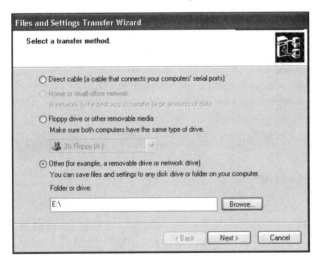

FIGURE A-4

Select the medium to use for transfer.

Select the option button that applies to the transfer medium you will use, and as necessary, identify the drive. Click Next to open the What Do You Want To Transfer? screen, as shown in Figure A-5.

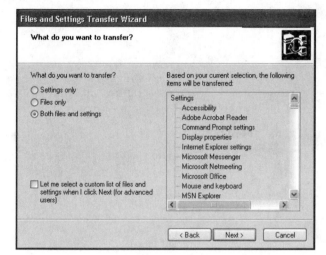

FIGURE A-5

Tell the wizard what you want to transfer.

Select to transfer only settings, only files, or both files and settings. You can also select custom files and settings by click the check box. The list on the right display what will be transferred based on your selection. Click Next to display the Install Programs On Your New Computer screen, suggesting some programs you may want to install on your new computer before transferring the settings.

Click Next to display the Collection In Progress screen, as shown in Figure A-6.

FIGURE A-6

The wizard collects information.

Click Finish.

After you finish installing Windows XP, follow these steps to transfer the files and settings to the new operating system:

Click the Start button, point to All Programs, point to Accessories, point to System Tools, and then click Files And Settings Transfer Wizard to start the wizard.

Click the Next button to open the Which Computer Is This? screen, and select the New Computer option.

3 Click Next to open the Do You Have A Windows XP CD? screen, as shown in Figure A-7.

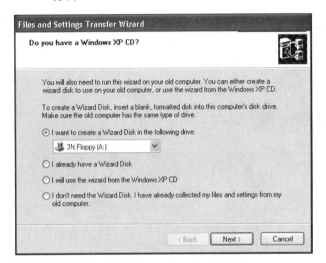

FIGURE A-7

Select the last option button.

4 Click the I Don't Need The Wizard Disk option, and then click Next to open the Where Are The Files And Settings? screen, as shown in Figure A-8.

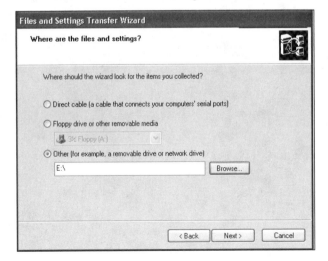

FIGURE A-8

Locate the files you saved.

5 Select an option to tell the wizard where the files are located, and click Next.

6 The wizard display the Transfer In Progress screen as it transfers the files.

Activating Windows XP

During the installation process, you are asked to activate your copy of Windows XP. Activation links the hardware in your computer with the product key associated with your copy of Windows XP. You connect to a special Microsoft web site to provide this information. If you don't activate Windows XP during installation, you have 30 days to do so. If you haven't activated by the end of that time, your system will stop working. In addition, if you try to install that same copy of Windows XP on another computer, you will be prompted to activate. This time, however, the activation will fail, and you will see a message that it is illegal to install a copy of Windows XP on more than one computer.

Note If you bought a new computer with Windows XP already installed on it, activation was probably done at the factory.

Activation is not the same thing as registration. You register your copy of Windows XP so that Microsoft can send you information and updates, but registration is optional. Activation is mandatory.

To activate Windows XP after you install and within the 30-day grace period, click the Start button, point to All Programs, and then click Activate Windows.

Installation Steps

As I said at the outset of this appendix, I'm not going to walk you through each step of the three ways you can install Windows XP. The Setup program will do that. Here, though, are the general steps in order:

1 Back up all your data files and/or run the Files And Settings Transfer Wizard.

2 Make a note of any Internet connection information. If you have a dial-up connection, you'll need your user account name, your password, the dial-up phone number, the name of your ISP's sending and receiving mail servers, and perhaps the name of their newsgroups server. If you have DSL, you may need to make a note of how the TCP/IP protocol is configured.

3 Be sure that all hardware connected to the computer is plugged in and turned on, including scanners, printers, and so on. If these components are all turned on, the Setup program will likely detect and install them automatically.

4 Disable antivirus software.

5 Run the Upgrade Advisor, as described earlier in this appendix.

6 Perform the upgrade, new installation, or clean installation.

7 If you ran the Files And Settings Transfer Wizard earlier, run it again to transfer the information to the new operating system.

8 As necessary, install any applications.

Reverting to a Previous Version of Windows

You cannot revert to a previous installation of Windows NT 4 Workstation or Windows 2000 Professional. You can revert to a previous installation of Window Me or Windows 98. To do so, follow these steps:

1 Click the Start button, and the click Control Panel to open Control Panel.

2 Click the Add Or Remove Programs link to open the Add Or Remove Programs dialog box.

3 Click Windows XP Uninstall.

4 Click the Change/Remove button to open the Uninstall Windows XP dialog box.

5 Click the Uninstall Windows XP option button, and then click the Continue button.

6 In the confirmation dialog box, click Yes. Windows XP is uninstalled, and your system restarts, running your previous version of Windows.

Glossary

Accessories

Windows XP comes with some extra, miniature programs called accessories. One such accessory is the Calculator program, for example. Another is the Solitaire game program.

Activation

A Windows XP security measure that insures you don't install Windows XP on more than one computer. Microsoft requires that each copy of Windows XP be activated within 30 days either over the phone or over the Internet.

Antivirus software

A program that can detect a computer virus and delete it.

Broadband connection

A fast Internet connection.

Burning

Copying a file to a CD.

Byte

A byte is an eight-character string of 0s and 1s, called binary digits or bits. The Windows operating system uses bytes to represent individual characters, such as the letter "w," and occasionally other information.

Cable modem

An Internet connection that uses your cable TV outlet. Information travels through a cable modem to and from your computer over a special channel on your cable signal.

Click

The process of pointing to an item and then clicking the mouse's left button is called clicking the item.

Client program

A client program is a software program that runs on your desktop or laptop computer but works with another program, called a server program, that runs on another computer. When you send e-mail, for example, you use an e-mail client program to create the message and deliver the message to a mail server. The mail server program then delivers the message to the recipient.

Compatibility Mode

A feature that sort of "tricks" a program into thinking it is running on the version of Windows for which it was created, rather than on Windows XP.

Compression

Decreasing the size of a file or a folder so that it takes up less space on a drive and transfers quicker.

Desktop

The Windows screen you see after you've started and logged onto your computer.

Digital Subscriber Line (DSL)

A broadband connection to the Internet that transfers information over a special part of your telephone line.

Directory

Another name for folder. Directories store files and other directories, or folders.

Disk

Your computer uses disks to store information in files. Hard disks (also called hard drives), floppy disks, and CDs are all disk storage devices. Disks are called disks because they're most often round platters.

Document

Windows calls the files you create with programs documents. In the case of a word-processor file, this term works pretty well. A letter, a report, or a customer proposal are all examples of either personal or business documents. Other times, the term doesn't apply quite as nicely, unfortunately. (Also see Multimedia Document.)

Domain

In essence, a domain is a network of computers connected to the Internet. Domain names appear in Internet addresses, including e-mail addresses and World Wide Web addresses. A domain can also be an administrative unit on a local area network.

Double-click

The process of pointing to an item and clicking the mouse's left button twice in a row quickly is called double-clicking the item.

E-mail

An electronic message, usually in the form of text, that you send from one computer to another. The Internet's most popular feature is e-mail, by the way.

File

A file is what Windows stores on your computer's storage devices—devices such as hard disks, floppy disks, and sometimes CDs. Interestingly, there are two separate varieties of files: document files store the information you create with a program such as a word processor; program files contain the instructions your computer needs to do the actual work.

File System

The way that Windows XP organizes and keeps track of the files stored on a hard disk. Windows XP supports three file systems: NTFS (the most secure), FAT (the old file system from the original DOS operating system), and FAT32 (a version of FAT that works for larger hard disks).

Folder

Windows uses folders to organize files on your disks. Most of the document files that you create, for example, will probably be stored in a folder named My Documents.

Hard disks

Large, fixed internal storage devices—typically located inside your personal computer or on a network server.

Hardware

Hardware is the physical gadgetry of your computer. Your monitor, disk, and printer are all hardware, for example.

Help and Support Center

The dramatically improved help system in Windows XP. You can use it to access the Microsoft Knowledge Base, get remote assistance from a friend or a colleague, step through troubleshooters to solve common problems, and more.

Hyperlink

A hyperlink is a piece of text or an image that points to another resource (usually on the Internet), such as a web page.

Internet

The Internet is a global network of smaller electronic networks. The Internet lets people across the world share information quickly and inexpensively, which is why some people refer to the Internet as the "information superhighway." A couple of the Internet's most popular services are electronic mail (e-mail) and the World Wide Web.

Internet Connection Firewall (ICF)

A program that's included with Windows XP and protects your computer system from unauthorized access over the Internet.

Internet service provider

An Internet service provider is a company that lets you connect your computer to their network. Because their network is part of the Internet, once you connect to this network, you're connected to the Internet and can use its resources. Microsoft provides its own Internet service provider, The Microsoft Network (MSN), but there are many others.

Integrated Services Digital Network (ISDN)

A type of Internet connection that is faster than dial-up modem but not as fast as a broadband connection. ISDN uses the phone line.

Local disk

A local disk is a disk storage unit that's inside the computer you're working on.

Local printer

A printer that is attached directly to your computer.

Logging off

Closing all the programs and files you've been using.

Logging on

Identifying yourself to the operating system.

Mail server

A mail server is the computer that does the work of delivering the e-mail messages you send to others and retrieving and storing the messages that other people send to you. Think of a mail server as the electronic equivalent of your local post office.

Microprocessor

The microprocessor is the part of your computer that actually executes the instructions given by the operating system and software programs. For example, if you tell a word processor to check the spelling in a document, it's actually the microprocessor that does the brainwork of comparing the words in your document to the words in a spelling dictionary.

Modem

A modem connects your computer and sometimes your television to a telephone line so that you can send or receive information. You can use a modem to connect to the Internet over a telephone line.

Monitor

A monitor is that television-screen like object that's connected to your computer.

Mouse

In Windows, you use a mouse to click and drag items. By clicking and dragging, you can often tell the operating system and programs what you want them to do.

Multimedia document

A multimedia document is a document that uses multiple media—sound, text, and pictures—for communicating information. Web pages are often multimedia documents, for example.

Network

A network is a group of computers that are connected together so that the computer users can share information and hardware.

Network disk

A network disk, also known as a network drive, is a disk that's inside another computer on the network you work on. To view or move information to and from a network disk, you use the network.

Network printer

A printer that is attached to a network.

Newsgroup

A newsgroup is a collection of messages—typically text messages—that people post to a central server so other people can read them. News-group messages closely resemble e-mail messages—in fact, you use the same basic process to create and post a newsgroup message as you do to create and send an e-mail message.

Notification area

The area at the far right of the taskbar that displays icons for currently running services. In previous versions of Windows, the notification area was known as the system tray or the status area.

Operating system

An operating system is the software that manages your computer's hardware. For example, it's really the operating system that prints documents on your printer. When you tell a program to print a letter, the program transmits a copy of the letter to the operating system, and it does the work of telling the printer how to print the letter.

Password

A password is a secret word or string of characters that you use to confirm your identity. When you log on to Windows, you supply a user name to identify yourself and a password to prove you're who you say you are.

Plug and Play

A specification that describes a device that a computer system can automatically configure when the device is connected to the system.

Port

An interface that allows a device and the computer to communicate.

Program

As the term is used in this book, a program is a piece of software you use to do your work or have fun. Your word processor, if you have one, is a program. Other popular programs include Microsoft's Excel spreadsheet program and Intuit's Quicken program.

RAM

An abbreviation for Random Access Memory. RAM is memory that temporarily stores information on your computer.

Recycle Bin

The Recycle Bin is a special folder that Windows uses to temporarily store the files you've deleted.

Remote Assistance

A Windows XP feature that lets you contact someone to help you with a computer problem and then allow that person to access your computer to solve the problem.

Search engines/service

A web site that maintains a searchable index, or list, of web pages.

Shortcut icons

Shortcut icons are clickable pictures. You typically use them to start programs and to open documents.

Software

Software provides instructions to your computer. Operating system software, for example, tells your computer's hardware what to do. Program software (which people also sometimes call application software) performs tasks such as word processing, accounting, and desktop publishing.

Start button

The Start button, which appears on the left side of the Taskbar, lets you start programs. You can also use it to stop Windows.

System Restore

A Windows XP feature that can restore the operating system to the settings that were being used when the system was running properly. You use System Restore when you can't boot into Windows XP.

Taskbar

The Taskbar is the bar at the bottom of the Windows desktop. The Taskbar provides the Start button, the Quick Launch buttons if you've chosen to display the Quick Launch toolbar, and buttons for any programs you've started. At the right end of the Taskbar is the notification area.

Theme

A group of settings that all together give the Windows XP desktop a certain look. These settings include the desktop background, colors, font styles and sizes, window sizes, sound events, mouse pointers, icons, and screen savers.

Toolbar

Some programs display rows of clickable buttons beneath their menu bars, which you can use to issue commands to a program. These rows of clickable buttons are called toolbars.

Virus

A malevolent program that can attach itself to your computer system without your knowledge or permission and wipe out all your work in less than a minute.

Web browser

A program that displays web pages. Windows XP has a built-in web browser, Internet Explorer.

Web server

When Windows requests a web page from the Internet, it makes its request to a web server, which is where the web documents are stored.

Web site

A web site is a collection of multimedia documents (web pages) connected by hyperlinks. People and companies publish web sites on the World Wide Web when they have more information to share than will fit comfortably in one document. For example, a company's web site might include one web page listing their products and services, one listing employment opportunities, one with hyperlinks to the latest news releases, and so on.

Window

A window (little "w") is just a rectangle that Windows (big "w") uses to display information.

Windows Messenger

An instant messaging program that's included with Windows XP.

Windows Update

A Windows XP feature that can automatically download and install updates to Windows when an administrator is logged on and the computer is connected to the Internet.

Winkey

The key on the keyboard that has a Windows logo on it.

Word processor

A word processor is a program that lets you create, save, and print text documents such as letters, school reports, and business documents.

World Wide Web

The World Wide Web is a collection of multimedia documents on the Internet that are connected with hyperlinks.

INDEX

display customization (using Control Panel), 206–219
  Appearance and Themes in, 206
  backgrounds in, 208
  color palette settings in, 217–219
  color schemes for, 215–216
  desktop customization using, 208–210
  dialog box customization using, 214–217
  Effects dialog in, 216–217
  icon customization in, 209–210
  power conservation settings in, 213–214
  screen resolution settings in, 217–219
  screen savers in, 210–213
  themes in, 207
  window element customization using, 214–217

document files, 32

domains, 2, 83

dot (.) in e-mail addresses, 83

double clicking the mouse, 6

dragging, 14, 27
  moving documents using, 43
  sliders and, 28

drop-down list boxes, 25–26, 28

DVDs
  image capture from, 231
  language selection in, 231
  playing, with Media Player, 229–233
  subtitles and closed captioning in, 231

E

Edit Menu, 19

editing text
  in Notepad, 133–134
  in WordPad, 140

Effects dialog, 216–217

e-mail, 5, 73, 83–99
  Address Book for, 96–99
  addresses for, 83, 84, 96–99
  at (@) and dot (.) in addresses for, 83
  attachments to, 94–96
  copies of (Cc line), 88

creating a message for, 88–91
deleting messages from Inbox, 92–93
delivering your messages to you, 91
domains in, 83
formatting a message for, 90–91
forwarding messages in, 94
Hypertext Markup Language (HTML) in, 89–90
mail servers for, 83, 87
Outlook Express setup for, 84–88
printer queues and, 65–67
reading messages in, 91–92
Remote Assistance invitation and, 188
replying to your messages in, 93–94, 104
saving copies of sent messages in, 104
Send button for, 89
Send/Receive button for, 91, 104
spell checking in, 89
Subject line in, 89
To box in, 88, 99
unsolicited (junk), 102
virus protection and, 153–154
in WordPad attachments, 142

emptying Recycle Bin, 46–47

Equalizer setting, Media Player, 230–231

erasing text, 27

Exit command, 10

Explorer Bar, 36

F

FAT32 file system, 255–257

Favorites menu for Web sites, in Internet Explorer, 114–115

fax modems, 147

Fax Service, 35

faxing, 147–150

File Allocation Table (FAT) file systems, 255–257

File Menu, 10, 19

file system, 31–52
  backing up files in, 48–49, 169, 173–175, 261
  Cleanup of unnecessary files in, 156–157